T0354082

Wherever you are on your journey to becoming the most effective reading teacher for the students in your care, Christina is a mentor you can count on. With the clarity and authenticity that comes from spending her days with learners, she has thoughtfully condensed a vast topic into six manageable chapters. Filled with her research-guided wisdom and resources for further study, she answers questions, big and small, about creating a thriving, equitable reading community. I wish I had Christina's book my first year of teaching, and I know that I will be turning to it often as I continue to learn about our most important work—nurturing joyful, passionate, critical readers.

Maria Walther
Author of *The Ramped-Up Read Aloud* and *Shake Up Shared Reading*

Finally! This book fills the needs of *all* reading teachers no matter what level they are at: preservice, early in their career, switching to a different grade, or those with decades of experience. It's ideal for a book study where teachers plan to review their practices with a "guide on the side," as Christina uses snippets from the classroom, research, and practical applications to answer your reading questions that cover the "why this matters" as well. Teaching reading today requires knowledge and skill; this text will give you the confidence and competence to increase your own expertise and knowledge. Ask a question, search the table of contents, and get started reading! You decide whether you read the book from cover to cover or seek out specific questions or chapters for starting points!

Fran McVeigh
Literacy Coach, Co-Moderator for #G2Great Chat, and
Academic Coordinator and Adjunct Faculty for Morningside University

Ten years ago we had Donalyn Miller's *The Book Whisperer* to guide us on how to awaken the reader in every child. Now, we have Christina Nosek's *Answers to Your Biggest Questions About Teaching Elementary Reading*, which reminds us of the important concepts that help to create a reading community that will support every student to see themselves as readers! As a building administrator, I want every teacher to have this book as we begin each school year to cultivate those reader leaders in our building! This will be a must-have resource for all teachers!

Lisa Castillo Guajardo
Principal of Mitchell Elementary, Houston, TX

Teaching reading is not a simple task; it's more like keeping the plates spinning in unison in an acrobatic performance. It requires that educators understand reading theory and models that support growing readers, have time to practice and hone their skills, and receive guidance on how to keep all the parts going. In *Answers to Your Biggest Questions About Teaching Elementary Reading*, Christina Nosek has provided up-to-date best practices that we should see in all classrooms. This comprehensive volume delivers on content while simultaneously coaching teachers to make effective decisions throughout the reading block. What I especially appreciate about this text is the focus on young (K–5) readers, placing them at the center of planning and teaching.

Sandy Brumbaum
Literacy Coach and Reading Recovery Teacher Leader

This extraordinary and teacher-friendly book is filled with rich, relevant, and practical guidance for anyone who teaches reading! Whether you are a new teacher or have been teaching for many years, the questions (and answers) that Christina poses in this book will help you create a reading classroom where all students can become joyfully literate humans.

Kelly Boswell
Educational Consultant and Author of *Every Kid a Writer*

From those percolating questions that keep you up at night to the curriculum presentations that require a justification of why the teaching of reading matters, this book is the compass that will steer you north. Validating, and centered on foundational understanding—in particular to the most vulnerable of children—this book holds social justice, agency, and lifelong learning at its core. A must-read for all teachers, time and time again! Christina Nosek makes the information digestible, relevant, and accessible to teachers and everyone who understands that the teaching and learning of reading goes way beyond the words on a page.

Lucía Rocha-Nestler
Senior Staff Developer and Literacy Consultant,
The Language and Literacy Collaborative

Imagine getting to be a fly on the wall of an exemplary teacher's classroom, watching reading instruction. Now imagine that you have a guidebook in front of you explaining why and how everything is happening, like the key on a map. This author is that teacher, and this book is that guide. *Answers to Your Biggest Questions About Teaching Elementary Reading* shares the whys and hows of great reading instruction in a classroom with clear examples and ample resources for those ready to dig deeper. It is an excellent resource for both new and veteran teachers wanting to make the best use of instructional time to help grow readers who will read for life, not just 20 minutes.

Jacqui Cebrian
Elementary Reading Specialist and Community Advocate for Book Access

Teaching young students reading is not easy, but Christina Nosek's important new book is here to help lay the foundation for educators. One of the critical components to powerful reading instruction is the *why* behind minilessons, strategies, conferences, small groups—what holds it all up? Christina walks readers through the why, the how, and offers a multitude of ideas to keep your reading instruction fresh, engaging, and student-focused. A book for reading teachers, yes, but also anyone working with teachers of elementary reading. I felt like Christina was sitting next to me, chatting and helping nudge my thinking about reading forward, and I'm excited for educators to get their hands on this valuable resource.

Matt Halpern
Education Consultant, Speaker, and Author

Christina Nosek is an educator with a passion for reflection, collaboration, and professional growth. Key questions anchor this book, and they are the questions that teachers of all experience levels grapple with, wonder about, and work to answer. With spotlights on community building, instruction, assessment, curriculum, and student agency, Christina weaves questions and answers with experience-based key commitments and practical strategies that will build your understanding of complex skills, your resources, and your confidence.

Melanie Meehan
Author of *Answers to Your Biggest Questions About Teaching Elementary Writing* and *Every Child Can Write*, co-author of *The Responsive Writing Teacher*

Christina Nosek expertly outlines and deeply explores holistic reading instruction that leads to curious, empowered, self-directed readers. If you want to learn practices that motivate and engage students in reading, structures that provide practical differentiation, instructional methods that work with a variety of classroom groupings, and assessments that serve your students and promote growth, then *Answers to Your Biggest Questions About Teaching Elementary Reading* is for you! I learned from this book, as well as found validation and inspiration in its chapters. I know you will too.

Mark Weakland
Literacy Coach, Consultant, and Author of *How to Prevent Reading Difficulties*

Thanks to Christina Nosek, my students will have a mentor literacy teacher with them at all times! She expertly guides us through the steps to create a robust community of lifelong readers, something our world desperately needs.

Susie Rolander
Bank Street College of Education

ANSWERS *to Your* BIGGEST QUESTIONS *About*

TEACHING ELEMENTARY READING

This is for you, Dad.

Our talks and walks are my favorite thing.

FIVE to THRIVE

ANSWERS *to Your* BIGGEST QUESTIONS *About*

TEACHING ELEMENTARY READING

Christina Nosek

CORWIN

For information:

Corwin
A SAGE Company
2455 Teller Road
Thousand Oaks, California 91320
(800) 233–9936
www.corwin.com

SAGE Publications Ltd.
1 Oliver's Yard
55 City Road
London, EC1Y 1SP
United Kingdom

SAGE Publications India Pvt. Ltd.
B 1/I 1 Mohan Cooperative
Industrial Area
Mathura Road, New Delhi 110 044
India

SAGE Publications
Asia-Pacific Pte. Ltd.
18 Cross Street #10–10/11/12
China Square Central
Singapore 048423

President: Mike Soules
Vice President and Editorial Director:
  Monica Eckman
Executive Editor: Tori Mello Bachman
Content Development Editor:
  Sharon Wu
Editorial Assistants: Nancy Chung
  and Nyle De Leon
Production Editor: Tori Mirsadjadi
Copy Editor: Amy Hanquist Harris
Typesetter: Integra
Proofreader: Talia Greenberg
Indexer: Maria Sosnowski
Cover Designer: Gail Buschman
Marketing Manager: Margaret O'Connor

Library of Congress Cataloging-in-Publication Data

Names: Nosek, Christina, author.
Title: Answers to your biggest questions about teaching elementary reading : five to thrive / Christina Nosek.
Description: Thousand Oaks, California : Corwin, 2022. | Series: Corwin literacy
Identifiers: LCCN 2021059386 | ISBN 9781071858011 (paperback) |
  ISBN 9781071876954 (epub) | ISBN 9781071876947 (epub) |
  ISBN 9781071876930 (adobe pdf)
Subjects: LCSH: Reading (Elementary) | Reading teachers--In-service training.
Classification: LCC LB1573 .N668 2022 | DDC 372.4--dc23/eng/20220106
LC record available at https://lccn.loc.gov/2021059386

This book is printed on acid-free paper.

22 23 24 25 26 10 9 8 7 6 5 4 3 2 1

Note From the Publisher: The author has provided video and web content throughout the book that is available to you through QR (quick response) codes. To read a QR code, you must have a smartphone or tablet with a camera. We recommend that you download a QR code reader app that is made specifically for your phone or tablet brand.

CONTENTS

3 WHAT ARE THE KEY INSTRUCTIONAL PRINCIPLES TO KNOW AND USE?   68

4 HOW DO I USE ASSESSMENT IN THE SERVICE OF STUDENTS?   102

5 HOW DO I SHIFT AGENCY TO STUDENTS, ENGAGING AND EMPOWERING THEM AS READERS?   126

6 WHERE DO I GO FROM HERE?   146

Visit the companion website at
resources.corwin.com/answerselementaryreading
for downloadable resources and video clips.

ACKNOWLEDGMENTS

This book is only possible because of all of the wise and forward-thinking literacy educators on whose shoulders I stand—starting with my own literacy methods professor at San Diego State University, Dr. Marva Cappello, and my mentor during my first year as a teacher, Midge Fuller, to the many others who have shaped my teaching practice since. From the workshops and professional development sessions led by the many thought leaders at The Teachers College Reading and Writing Project, to the detailed information about texts and readers in the writings of Fountas & Pinnell and the continued work of the many educators and researchers whose work I follow on a regular basis (many of which are listed as Great Resources throughout this book)—thank you.

On a more personal-professional note: To my #G2Great mentors, Writing Zone friends, friends from NCTE, Doing the Work group, and all others who push me and value equity in literacy education as much as I do, I am deeply grateful for the continued fuel you provide that keeps this fire lit. I may not see you or even get to chat with you often, but your impact and influence are always with me on this journey. Tori, a huge *thank you* to you and Corwin for believing in me. I thoroughly enjoyed our 5 a.m. conversations and this entire process.

On a very personal-professional note: An enormous thank you goes to my former partner in literacy coaching—reading specialist extraordinaire, Angie Lew. Angie, thank you for taking the time to read and offer feedback on multiple paragraphs and sections of this book as it developed. A huge thank you also goes to my teaching colleagues who helped in this process: Haley Harrier, Ann Kwolek, Stephanie Han, and of course my #DreamTeam, Katie and Laura. Jim, Jenn, Katie K., and Molly—I am always grateful for our continued teacher-talk and non-teacher-talk over good food and drink! Teaching is an amazing calling. It's made even better when I get to do it every single day with past and present colleagues who I also get to call my dearest friends.

On a strictly personal note: Alternating drafting, revising, biking, yoga, strength training, and drafting/revising again on the regular was necessary in this writing process. A massive message of gratitude goes out to my most turned-to Peloton instructors: Christine, Denis, Sam, Leeanne, Ben, Jess K., Kristin, Chelsea, and Matty. I would be a very different person and writer without your consistent words and encouragement on the bike and mat. What you do makes a difference. And thank you to Robin in my Friday 6 a.m. Peloton riders group for lending me your pedals when one of mine broke! You saved my ability to write for a couple of critical weeks there! *I am* a teacher–writer. *I can* concurrently write and teach. *I will* make a difference. *I do* this because I'm called to—and I love it! #WriterChris13

Finally, to my family and friends near and far, thank you for your support and encouragement while I completely buried myself in writing this book on top of working as a full-time classroom teacher. It's now time to relax and enjoy! Let's grab a glass of California white or Pennsylvania red, toast around the fire, cheer on our SJ Sharks, chase Michelin stars, enjoy great conversation at early dinners, linger in museums, belt it out at concerts, hike out in nature, go on that trip, FaceTime across the ocean, frolic in the tulips, walk the dog (especially my favorite boy Prince), solve the world's problems, and just spend more time together. I love you all.

PUBLISHER'S ACKNOWLEDGMENTS

Corwin gratefully acknowledges the contributions of the following reviewers:

Connie Obrochta
Reading Recovery Teacher Leader, Reading Interventionist

Viviana Tamas
AIS Reading Teacher/Literacy Coach K–5

ABOUT THE AUTHOR

 **Christina Nosek** is a passionate classroom teacher of 20 years and a literacy education staff developer in her time away from the classroom. She equally loves teaching children and supporting teachers in developing their classroom reading and writing communities. Her past roles include reading specialist and literacy coach. When she is not working in education, she's enjoying life in the San Francisco Bay Area. This is her second book for teachers.

While organizing and cleaning out my new classroom prior to the start of my first year of teaching in 2002, I uncovered a familiar book. It was white with a thick blue border, a photograph of a cocker spaniel on the cover. Memories flooded back. I immediately recognized the book as one of the reading textbooks from my elementary school days in the 1980s. I couldn't believe the book was still around.

I remembered holding that book as a 9-year-old student, pretending to follow along as other kids in class read aloud from it. Rather than actually following along as the teacher expected, I counted the paragraphs to figure out which one would be mine to read aloud. I practiced my paragraph over and over again in my head as my classmates read aloud. I remembered my classmate Barry, who stuttered as he read, and the laughter from a couple of other kids in class. When I think about it, I still intensely feel anger toward the teacher for putting Barry through that. However, as a teacher myself now, I wonder if my teacher back then knew the pain she was causing—perhaps she was just following directions from above or teaching the way she learned in school because she just never learned otherwise.

A few weeks later, as I flipped through my school's more current basal reader, I compared the two books side by side. Indeed, not much had changed in the basal reader world since the 1980s. Both books featured a collection of stories with comprehension questions after each one. Most teachers at my school at the time did not strictly follow the basal program page by page. Rather, they referred to it now and again as a few good stories were included, but they primarily relied on their classroom libraries, the school bookroom, and collaboration with each other to develop their reading instructional plans. They knew that encouraging choice in reading and building high-interest classroom libraries were the cornerstones of building a classroom reading community.

That first year, I was mentored by an incredible teacher in the classroom next door: Midge Fuller. Midge, a veteran teacher of over 30 years at the time, supported my literacy instruction by watching me teach and providing feedback. She often helped me practice and refine my guided reading instruction and excitedly shared new titles in children's literature.

In the winter of that year, Midge brought me along to a professional development session presented by Katie Wood Ray at a local college. I remember being mesmerized by Ray's words and passion for teaching. On the car ride home, after watching the session in a large theater filled with other like-minded educators, Midge talked about the reciprocity of reading and writing, named a few other literacy thought leaders I should read, and emphasized that learning as a teacher never stops. It's a careerlong endeavor—a magical one that I was fortunate to embark upon! That moment was a turning point for me. I knew my path forward in education was to continually learn everything I could about literacy teaching and learning.

I wish all new teachers had someone like Midge to lead them onto their path of continual learning and growth. Although I only worked with Midge for one year, her impact remains with me. Midge's example and mentorship as a literacy teacher guided me toward my master's degree in equity in literacy education. It led me to my ongoing membership in the National Council of Teachers of English, and most importantly, it keeps me continually reading professional texts and refining my practice to this day. If you do not have a teaching mentor like Midge to give you a starting point on your literacy learning journey—or if you are striving to be like Midge by supporting the work of continual teacher growth—this book is for you. If you do have a Midge in your life, perhaps you're picking up this book to continue to refine your practice.

WHY DO WE READ?

The first time I walked into Midge's third-grade classroom to observe her teach, it was reading time. Lamps around the room created a sense of warmth. Instrumental music played at low volume; the soft light and the background music fostered a sense of calm. Midge sat at her horseshoe-shaped table with four students, surrounded by books and notebooks. Three of the readers and Midge were all intently listening to one student's thoughts on a strategy he just tried. A few students were huddled together in a corner, all holding a copy of the same book while deep in discussion. Others were sitting at their desks or in large bean bag chairs, independently reading from their book boxes. I saw students laughing, deeply engaging in conversation, jotting notes, reading with eyes glued to the page, and Midge not leading but *facilitating* a reading strategy group. All at the same time in this one reading session, there was *reading to learn*, *reading to be entertained*, and *reading to grow* taking place.

The reasons for reading in school should mirror the reasons we read outside of school.

In the world outside of school, people read for many reasons, including to do these things:

- Find understanding
- Acquire information
- Challenge thinking
- Learn how to do something
- Relax and let go
- Laugh and enjoy
- Socialize and connect

Midge provided students opportunities to read for different purposes in her classroom. Unfortunately, and for various reasons, reading inside of school often does not resemble the reading that we do in the world outside of the school building. In order to set students up for success, the world inside of school should resemble what they will be asked to do outside school. As in Midge's classroom, students need to have opportunities to laugh, learn, and grow during their reading time.

HOW IS TEACHING READING DIFFERENT TODAY?

Reading instruction has evolved in exciting ways over time. In addition to understanding the important roles of word recognition, fluency, and comprehension in the process of reading, teachers of reading now also know the impact of many other factors in reading instruction and learning, thanks to the research and teaching of many scholars and educators in the field. Teachers of reading now know the following facts:

- High volume of reading (minutes read plus words read) plays a critical role in a child's reading growth, including

  - Vocabulary acquisition (Krashen, 1989; Nagy et al., 1987; Nation & Coady, 1988)
  - Building background knowledge (McVee et al., 2005; Ozuru et al., 2009)

  - Increasing achievement (Allen et al., 2015; Allington, 2012; Anderson et al., 1988)

- A one-size-fits-all approach does not work. Reading teachers now strive for equity and responsive instruction. At the classroom level, equity refers to every student having the right to be taught in a way that serves their own individual strengths and needs as opposed to every student being given the same thing. We can achieve equity, or start to work toward it, when we teach responsively following the strengths that already exist in each of our students (Muhammad, 2020).

- Early reading foundational skills of listening comprehension and decoding (see *The Simple View of Reading*, Gough & Tunmer, 1986) play a key role in a child's reading development. While this has been known for decades, recently there has been a greater focus in ensuring all readers receive the needed instruction in these critical foundational skills.

- In addition to decoding and listening comprehension, many other factors play a role to encompass the active view of reading. One of these factors is active self-regulation, which includes motivation, engagement, and executive function skills (Duke & Cartwright, 2021).

- Skilled literacy educators now seek to help all students engage in productive struggle to grow. The focus on back-to-basics instruction instead of embracing intellectual grapple and curiosity has hurt many students, especially students learning English as an additional language. The work of Zaretta Hammond (2015) tells us that a culturally responsive pedagogy includes ensuring that all of our students receive instruction to meet and appropriately challenge their intellectuality.

- Our society has access to more information—and *mis*information—than we ever have before due to widespread and constant online access. An important part of reading instruction now includes spending instructional time to support students in critically evaluating and reading sources and information, both online and off.

- Finally, the way literacy educators view texts children read is vastly different than in years past. In fact, the way text is defined is even different! Text can include a traditional book, comic book, graphic text, online article, video, images, audiobooks and files, and more! The one commonality among all of these types of text is that students need to learn how to decipher, understand, and even evaluate them.

WHAT IF I'M TEACHING A VIRTUAL, HYBRID, OR OTHER NONTRADITIONAL MODEL?

During the first 10 months of the Covid-19 pandemic, I heard many people repeat the phrase, "Good teaching is good teaching no matter which model you use." As someone who has now been a classroom teacher in a prepandemic traditional setting, full virtual setting, hybrid setting (students in-person and at a distance concurrently), and again in a full-class/in-person setting with masking precautions in place, I can tell you it's true. Good teaching is good teaching—but making it happen is no easy feat when quick, unexpected adjustments need to be made. However, putting three guiding questions at the forefront of your decision-making will help you make the most of teaching in any setting.

1 *What constitutes good teaching?*
   Good teaching always involves following the lead of your students before all else. In times of uncertainty, keep your students' strengths and needs at the forefront of your decision-making. Also keep in mind that those strengths and needs at any given time may change. Good teaching also accounts for social-emotional considerations. When social-emotional needs are met, students are more likely to engage in learning. Good teaching also prioritizes essentials. For example, when my school quickly switched to a virtual model of teaching in March of 2020, I simply did not have enough time in the allotted teaching day to do everything I once did in the classroom. Yet I did make time for the essentials I knew were important for my students' reading development: to read aloud and implement supported independent reading every day.

2 *What do my students need right now?*
   As a teacher of reading, and of all subjects in elementary school, keep in mind that you are tasked with teaching the children you serve, not necessarily teaching every page of the curriculum. Sometimes, adjustments need to be made. Oftentimes, the social-emotional needs of your students will outweigh the academic requirements of the curriculum. Always asking what it is that your students need right now will help guide you in making those needed adjustments when you're called to make a change in setting or teaching model.

3 *Considering the time constraints I have, what are some things I can let go of?*
   When asked how I fit it all in, my response is the same: I don't fit it all in. As a teacher, you will constantly consider what you value and then make time for those things accordingly. If something is not valuable, consider this as your permission to let it go. To identify if something is valuable or not, I recommend evaluating the task or activity with the following two questions:

- Are my students learning something valuable that transfers to their independent reading?
- Do my students find joy or fulfillment in this activity?

If the answer is *no* to either one of these questions, the task or activity at hand might not be the best use of your reading instructional time. It's true that, as a teacher, you will make time for what you value most. While you will not be able to decide everything, especially teaching in times of turmoil or unrest, you do have control and decision-making power over quite a bit.

HOW SHOULD I USE THIS BOOK?

I hope you turn to this book in the way that I turned to Midge so many years ago. Every time I had a burning question or needed support in my practice, I sought out Midge. Oftentimes, Midge gave me some information to get me going but then recommended a book I should read to learn more, a teaching method I should try, or a classroom language choice that was new to me. Midge gave me enough to get me started and then guided me toward learning more on my own. This is exactly what I hope this book will do for you and the teachers you work with.

This book is not a curriculum, a sequence of lessons, or a how-to. Rather, it is a collection of the most important concepts you need to know with answered questions that comprise the foundation of the reading classroom. Reading this book will not give you a script to follow but rather a starting point if you're new to teaching reading. It may also provide philosophies and methodologies for you to consider if you are a veteran whose goal is to focus on authentic reading instruction in your classroom practice.

You will find helpful features throughout, such as practical teaching tips, important principles to keep in mind, terms to know, great resources to help you learn more, photos from actual classrooms, and QR codes that will take you to short, explanatory videos. Keep in mind, this book was written during the ongoing Covid-19 pandemic. All photos of students are from classrooms where masking procedures were in place. But the masking didn't stop staff and students from the important work of teaching and learning!

Short stories from my own classroom and classrooms of my current and former colleagues help illustrate certain points throughout the book—to show you where theory and research actually fit into real classroom practice.

If you are a new teacher, this book might be a reminder of practices you learned in your teacher education program. It might also give you some new things to consider. It is likely that much of the information in the book will be new to you. I recommend picking one area to start as your focus. Perhaps you will want to focus on building a reading community first. In that case, start with Chapter 1. If you feel you need a refresher on key instructional principles, you might start with Chapter 3. Allow your needs at this moment in time to be your guide. Throughout the book, I will guide you to other resources and thought leaders in reading education to learn more. This book will be your jumping-off point, not your end point.

If you are a veteran teacher, this book might be a reminder of best practices and why you do what you do for your readers in the classroom. It might also introduce you to a few new ideas and methods in reading instruction. After all—as Midge instilled in me so many years ago—as teachers, we never stop learning.

If you are a literacy coach, this book might be used as a reference for your own work or as a book study to lead with the teachers you serve. It will especially help you serve the new teachers you work with.

If you are an administrator, this book will help you know what good reading instruction looks like. Please use it to positively support and encourage your teachers in creating thriving and equitable reading communities and in planning and delivering effective reading instruction.

If you are a teacher educator, this book is a good starting point for your preservice teachers to start thinking about five guiding questions from which to ground their reading practice in their future classrooms and their current student teaching assignments. Additionally, this book is a collection of accessible starting points for new or soon-to-be-new teachers.

If you are a preservice teacher, thank you for joining our profession! You are our future. Perhaps you are even one of our future literacy leaders! This book is your starting point to learning all about how to best create a reading classroom to serve the strengths and needs of your future students. In the pages ahead, you will start to learn the basics of reading instruction and where to go next. I am so glad that you are here for the journey!

WHAT ARE THE FIVE THINGS I NEED TO KNOW RIGHT NOW?

Each of the chapters ahead focuses on one big guiding question that you need to know right now to get you started. There are then seven to 12 subquestions answered under the guiding questions.

Five Guiding Questions

1. How Do I Build and Maintain a Reading Community?
2. How Do I Structure, Organize, and Plan My Reading Instruction?
3. What Are the Key Instructional Principles to Know and Use?
4. How Do I Use Assessment in the Service of Students?
5. How Do I Shift Agency to Students, Engaging and Empowering Them as Readers?

You might decide to read the chapters in the order presented, or you might decide to read what you need in the moment and come back as necessary.

The most important thing you need to know right now is that you are on a continual learning journey to be the kind of reading teacher who values your own learning because you know your students' learning depends on it. This book might be your first stop or perhaps your 10th stop on that path. It certainly is not your last. By picking up this book, you already know and value your own growth as a reading teacher. As Midge instilled in me so many years ago, learning is a careerlong endeavor, and it's a magical one!

HOW DO I BUILD AND MAINTAIN A READING COMMUNITY?

Ms. Bodin, a third-year teacher, felt confident with the teaching of reading in the classroom. She implemented a thoughtful and intentional mix of whole-group and small-group instruction, and she made it a point to confer with students daily. After a month into the school year, she was pleased to see individual student growth in many areas of reading. However, she knew something was missing. The growth in her class was individual. She couldn't help but feel that her classroom full of individual readers wasn't yet actively coming together as a community of readers. While her students could sustain independent reading in an environment with different forms of teacher instructional support, she realized that her students rarely talked with each other about reading. Plus, there was not much excitement around the act of reading, the books themselves, or the other types of reading material. Lots of proficient, skills-based reading was taking place, but the magic and ongoing pulse of a thriving, living reading community was missing.

The pages ahead are for Ms. Bodin and others who are seeking to build and maintain a thriving and ever-growing community of readers in the classroom. All that is involved in this ongoing work will be introduced and explained. As you read the pages ahead, you will learn that before you can build a *community* of readers you need to identify and value the identities of all *individual members* of that community. In community building, there is an emphasis on celebrating all identities and placing a focus on lots of whole-group, small-group, and partner talk.

Eight of Your Biggest Questions About Building and Maintaining a Reading Community

1. What is my own identity as a reader?

2. How do I get to know my students as readers?

3. How can I support my students in building and celebrating their identities as readers?

4. How can I make reading relevant for my students?

5. How do I start to build and maintain a reading community?

6. How can I set up conditions to foster authentic student talk and collaboration?

7. How do I involve families and caregivers in their child's reading life?

8. How can I continually work to make my teaching culturally and linguistically relevant?

What Is My Own Identity as a Reader?

WHAT IS READING IDENTITY?

Reading identity can be defined as, but not limited to, how you view yourself as a reader: What are your reading habits, preferences, choices, self-perceptions, and ways of thinking you apply when you approach reading? Reading identities are not fixed. They grow and change over time, based on different factors.

WHY DO TEACHERS NEED TO RECOGNIZE AND NAME THE PARTS THAT MAKE UP THEIR OWN READING IDENTITY?

Before you can get to know and support students in building positive identities as readers, it is important to clearly understand your own reading identity. Understanding and making the effort to grow your own reading identity will enable you to not only empathize with your student readers, but it will also better position you to support students in recognizing and growing their own reading identities.

HOW CAN I GET TO KNOW AND CONTINUE TO GROW MY OWN READING IDENTITY?

To understand your own reading identity a little better, answer the questions in the left column of the following table (Getting to Know My Own Reading Identity). My answers appear in the right column. It is likely that, although you and I both work in elementary education and are fluent, experienced readers, our answers will be quite different. It will be the same for your students; they'll likely all have different reading identities.

Getting to Know My Own Reading Identity	Christina's Answers to These Questions (Likely Different From Yours)
• What are some of your reading memories and turning points?	• I actually did not like reading or even view myself as a reader until my middle school librarian did a book talk about the *Nancy Drew* series. This was a turning point for me.
• What do you usually read (genres, topics, authors)?	• I usually read nonfiction on a topic I am interested in exploring further. For example, I used to read quite a bit on road biking, but I no longer road bike. I now read a lot of food magazines and blogs.
• Where and when do you read, and why do you read there?	• I do a lot of reading in my kitchen or backyard, usually in the early evenings. When I have time after school, I find comfort reading in these places.
• Spy on yourself as a reader. What do you notice?	• When I sat down to read just now, I noticed these things: ○ I oriented myself to the text by scanning the entire article before I started reading. ○ I reread a particular section a couple of times when I wasn't understanding what the author wrote. I even needed to Google an unfamiliar cooking term.
• How do you authentically respond to your reading?	• Lately, I've been cooking! I've been following directions of the food blogs I'm reading. Sometimes, I decide to change a few things in the recipes.

SHARING YOUR READING IDENTITY WITH STUDENTS

"I remember I didn't fall in love with reading or view myself as a reader at all until I discovered the Nancy Drew *mysteries when I was in sixth grade."* Sharing this piece of my reading life in conversation with students during a morning meeting a few years ago led us to a bigger conversation about the power of finding an engaging reading series. Later in the day during reading time, I noticed a few students gathered in the classroom library browsing through our "first in a series" book basket.

When you are open about sharing your own reading identity, your students will be more likely to share theirs as well. In addition to building trust and a relationship with students, doing this also normalizes imperfection. When you share your reading life with students, be sure to share both your successes and challenges. Think about how you answered the Getting to Know My Own Reading Identity questions and how you might authentically share some of your responses with your students.

DETERMINING YOUR BELIEFS ABOUT READING INSTRUCTION

As a teacher of reading, your core beliefs about reading instruction will become a part of your reading identity. These core beliefs about reading instruction will guide your relationship with students, your communication with caregivers, and your instructional decisions. These beliefs will be the foundation from which your reading community is built.

Take a moment to finish these prompts to start to determine your core beliefs about reading instruction:

- All students need _____ to grow as readers.
- All students should feel _____ about reading.
- All students should have access to _____.
- Reading instructional decisions are based on _____.

Which of these common shared beliefs about reading instruction resonate with you? What would you add?

Common Shared Beliefs About Reading Instruction

- All students deserve to view themselves as readers.
- All students should be able to see themselves in the books in their classroom.
- All students should have access to many books they can read and want to read.
- All students have the right to the instruction they need to continually grow as readers.
- Decisions about reading instruction are based on the strengths and needs of students through formative assessment, not necessarily the scope and sequence of a program.

Notes

How Do I Get to Know My Students as Readers?

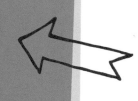

In our numeric, standardized-test, data-driven system, it is critically important to look beyond the numbers, letters, and labels to make an effort to understand your students' identities as readers. Understanding students' habits, motivations, and how they view themselves as readers will empower you to know who they are individually and as members of your developing reading community. This positions you better as a teacher who can fully support each of them.

LOOK BEYOND TRADITIONAL DATA

Take a look at these two sets of data about a young reader named Janelle. The left column lists Janelle's standardized test scores and summative assessment data. The right column shows a portion of Janelle's reading autobiography that she wrote at the beginning of the school year.

District Data Collection Assessments at the Beginning of the School Year	A Portion of Janelle's Reading Autobiography From the Beginning of the School Year
• Reading at Independent level M • Close to meeting minutes requirements on the computerized reading program • *Proficient* range in spring standardized testing from the year prior	*I loved it when my grandma used to read to me when I was little. We used to always choose books together. Then reading just became boring. I had to read the books my teachers gave me even if I didn't like them. This summer my friend started reading the* Mindy Kim *books. I started reading one and loved it! I hope I can read the* Mindy Kim *books in this class.*

What do you know and wonder about Janelle as a reader based on the left column? Are there actionable steps you can take to help her grow? Now consider these questions after reading the right column.

For example, based on the data in both columns, I might seek out more books similar to the *Mindy Kim* series and offer them to Janelle in a book stack, telling her, "These books made me think of you because you like the *Mindy Kim* series. When you're done with those books, you might consider trying some of these."

GET TO KNOW STUDENTS' READING AND PERSONAL IDENTITIES

Getting to know your students as readers is an ongoing process that will last the entire school year. Identities are not fixed. They change and evolve over time, based on different experiences. Ongoing reading conferences and classroom observations during reading time are a vital component of learning about your students' reading identities (conferences will be discussed in depth in Chapter 3). Additionally, the following tools will help you better understand your students' reading identities.

STUDENT INTEREST SURVEY

It takes a number of reading conferences, small-group sessions, and observations at the beginning of the year to really get to know a reader. However, one tool that can be used right away is an interest survey (K–1, 2–3, and 4–5 Student Interest Surveys can be found in Appendixes A, B, and C). At the beginning of the school year and then once again after winter break, invite students to fill out an interest survey to learn some of their interests, likes, dislikes, and reading experiences. Asking students to fill out the survey at two different points in the year will help you learn how their interests and preferences grow and change over time. Additionally, inviting students to reflect on how their interests have changed over time by reading their two surveys side by side will support them in continuing to learn more about who they are as readers. Take a look at Janelle's reading interest surveys from the beginning and middle of the school year.

Janelle's interests and identity as a reader have evolved over the course of a few months in school.

READING AUTOBIOGRAPHY

Another way to get to know students as readers is to invite them to create their own reading autobiographies.

- In the lower grades, this can involve drawing a couple of pictures of themselves reading. Ask students to draw a time when reading made them happy and also a time when reading made them feel sad or frustrated.
- In the upper grades, this might include creating a timeline of reading memories and turning points.

Students can do this at the beginning of the school year and then add to it or revise it every couple of months. It's a great way to really understand what your student readers value and what doesn't work for them.

TEACHER OBSERVATION SURVEY

It's also useful to keep an ongoing observation survey and conferring notes (more on conferring notes in Chapter 3) for each student. This observation survey is a great way to remember and keep track of "noticings" and wonderings about a student reader over time. Take a look at the first page of the observation survey Janelle's teacher filled out over the first few weeks of school. The observation survey will not only help you inform your teaching over time, but it will also inform your discussions with your students and their caregivers about their progress. A blank two-page Teacher Observation Survey can be found in Appendix D.

By jotting observation notes while Janelle was reading, her teacher was able to get to know her better and inform a few instructional decisions.

Teacher Observation Survey

Student Name __Janelle__   Dates _9/1 – 9/21_

Book Choice Observations

Date 9/1	Date 9/3	Date 9/6
• Rainbow fairy book, but doesn't seem interested	- Spent a lot of time browsing library. Asked for Mindy Kim *order Mindy Kim books*	- Started reading a nonfiction book on horses

Date 9/8	Date 9/14	Date 9/21
• Mindy Kim books arrived • Picked two to read • Really engaged in first	• On her third Mindy Kim book!	• Still on Mindy Kim series *I need to seek out a similar series*

Reading Engagement & Stamina Observations

Date 9/1	Date 9/3	Date 9/6
• seems distracted • holding book but looking around	• seems to have trouble picking a book • not interested in books I have.	• more engaged • Read for 12 minutes before looking for another book

Date 9/8	Date 9/14	Date 9/21
• Mindy Kim books made all the difference! • Read for 20 straight minutes!	• Read for entire time!! Very engaged	• Still engaged!

Answers to Your Biggest Questions About Teaching Elementary Reading, Chapter 1 2   Christina Nosek 2022

Keep in Mind

Interest and observation surveys and reading autobiographies are great ways to get to know students, but they cannot replace frequent, ongoing reading conferences where you spend time authentically talking with your students. See Chapter 3 for more on reading conferences.

How Can I Support My Students in Building and Celebrating Their Identities as Readers?

Equity

Each of your students has many reading strengths! Push yourself to create an ongoing list of students' strengths as readers. Point out these strengths to your students.

It's often easy to celebrate and compliment your voracious readers in class. However, every student has a multitude of strengths in addition to areas of growth as readers. All of your students are consistently doing something strategic and will benefit from feedback to help them continue to grow. It is your job to not only celebrate your students in their present identity as readers but also to set up conditions in the classroom where they can also support and encourage each other in growing their reading identities.

APPROACHES FOR CELEBRATING ALL READING IDENTITIES

- Adopt an asset-based approach. First, look for what a student is doing well and build upon that before stepping in to offer next steps. When you notice a student doing something new or positive as a reader, let them know what they are doing so they will continue to do it.
- Reframe language to center your students. When complimenting students on their reading, rather than using language such as "I like _____" to let them know what they are doing well, reframe it to make it specifically about what they are doing. Doing this makes the new reading behavior or strategy about the *student* instead of about pleasing you as the teacher. To make it even more powerful, let your students know *why* it will benefit them as readers. Try out these simple swaps to get started.

Instead of . . .	Say . . .
"I like how you are sitting in a good spot to read."	"You chose a great spot to read today. When you choose a spot like this, away from distraction, you will be able to better focus on your reading."
"I like how you sounded out each part of that tricky word."	"You just sounded out each part of that tricky word. This is one of your strategies you can try each time you come to a tricky word in your reading."

- Embrace the power of *yet*. In her 2014 TED Talk, *The Power of Believing You Can Improve*, psychologist Carol Dweck explains the power of believing in the notion of *yet*. Rather than naming what students aren't doing, instead use an asset-based approach to identify next steps. For example, rather than thinking, "These students are not stopping to think while they read," reframe your thinking to say, "It appears these students are not stopping to think while they read quite *yet*. What can I do to support them in this next step as readers?"

- Make successes and next steps public. Many teachers have started inviting students to publicly share success as well as areas they're working on to improve. Doing this normalizes that all readers still have things to work on.
- Provide students ample time to talk about their reading lives and preferences with you and each other. By providing this time, you let students know that you value what it is that they have to say about reading. This time can be planned and included in lessons or found in the in-between moments: waiting in line, transitioning from one activity to the next, or even when a spare minute pops up. The more opportunities students have to talk with you and each other about what they believe, prefer, and value as readers, the more their reading identities will grow and your community will continue to blossom.
- Celebrate and display student reading preferences. A simple yet highly effective way to honor student reading preferences is to invite them to share their favorite weekly or monthly reads with the whole class. This can be accomplished in a couple of ways. One way to do this is through verbal sharing in a morning meeting or at the end of reading time. Another way is to display images of students holding their favorite books on a bulletin board. In my own classroom, we take new pictures at the end of every month for display on a bulletin board. Students love sharing their monthly favorites and seeing what books their friends have enjoyed as well.

Great Resource

Trusting Readers: Powerful Practices for Independent Reading by Jennifer Scoggin and Hannah Schneewind (Heinemann, 2021)

COMMUNITY

Kate and Dash hold up their favorite reads from September.

How Can I Support My Students in Building and Celebrating Their Identities as Readers?

17

How Can I Make Reading Relevant for My Students?

By fifth grade, Lali had developed many masking mechanisms to hide the fact that she wasn't reading during independent reading time. She was skilled in holding a book to create the appearance of reading, offering to help around the classroom to avoid reading, and talking a big game to convince the adults around her of almost anything. I'll admit, I did not catch on for the first couple of weeks of school. When I finally did, I asked her to tell me more about how she viewed her reading life. "Reading is just boring, Ms. Nosek. Why would I want to spend my time reading?" Lali clearly did not yet view reading as a relevant part of her life.

Making reading relevant for students is all about keeping their reading and personal identity at the forefront of planning. As you read on, you'll see that working to keep reading relevant for Lali was what eventually supported her in viewing herself as a reader.

Five Key Principles of Reading Relevancy

1. Book access
2. Personal identity
3. Timeliness
4. Varied reading material
5. Authentic response

BOOK ACCESS

Students should have access to a large number of books that they can read and want to read. In order to continually support students in viewing themselves as readers, your first step is to keep your classroom library updated with books that interest all of them. Students will not read if they do not have access to a wide range of appealing reading material. When they finish one book or one stack of books, students need to know that many more await. Tips for building your classroom library on a teacher-friendly budget can be found in Chapter 2 (see Library, p. 47).

PERSONAL IDENTITY

Students should have access to books where they can see themselves, their peers, their community members, and all of humanity reflected. Additionally, these books should fall within a wide range of topics, authors, and genres. Lali did not view herself as a reader until she found Sharon Draper's *Blended* (2018). "This is the best book I've ever read. The character is mixed, just like me! I need more books like this."

Representation matters. In Lali's case, seeing herself in a book was the turning point in viewing herself as a reader.

TIMELINESS

Students should have access to books that are current—written for and about their generation, the issues they face, and the world they currently live in. Books written decades ago may not universally engage readers of today; even if your school purchased 30 copies of Gardiner and Sewell's *Stone Fox*, for example, and every fourth-grade class has read it since it was published in 1980, consider whether that's a book that will truly engage the readers in your care and whether its language and themes have stood up to the test of time.

While books should not simply be discarded because of their age, they should be critically examined. Ask yourself some questions before deciding to keep a book on the shelf.

Equity

All students should see themselves, their families, and their community members represented in the words and pictures of books included in your classroom library and read alouds.

Questions to Ask When Weeding Books From the Classroom Library

- Who in my classroom might find this book relatable?
- Is there a universal theme in this book that may be offered in a more modern context?
- Will the children in my classroom see themselves and their families in this book?
- Are there problematic representations or stereotypes in this book?
- Is the book in poor physical condition (yellowing pages, missing parts, etc.)?

There is no single book that will universally engage all readers. It is important for teachers of reading to remain informed about children's literature and to always keep readers in mind. You might consider putting books away one year, then bringing them back out the next, depending on the readers you teach. Places to keep informed about children's literature can be found in Appendix E.

VARIED READING MATERIAL

Students will read more and view reading as relevant when they understand that reading involves so much more than picking up traditional physical books. Our world—and the way we access information and entertainment in it—is rapidly evolving in an exciting way; therefore, the teaching of reading has to evolve as well.

To make reading relevant for your students, it's important to keep an open and evolving sense of acceptable reading material. Students should have access to reading material other than traditional physical books; audiobooks, texts in digital formats, articles, magazines, comic books, web pages, and other types of reading material are all valuable and worthwhile.

Keep in Mind

Many children start to view themselves as readers when they first fall for a comic book or graphic novel. Highly visual texts offer children the opportunity to think and stretch themselves as readers just as much as print-only texts. If a child loves reading graphic texts, encourage it! In fact, seek out more to add to your classroom library!

AUTHENTIC RESPONSE

Authentic response to reading refers to the unsolicited reaction a person has during or after reading. When students' authentic responses to their reading are honored, reading will become more relevant. Think about it: As adult readers, we read to laugh, to learn, to grow, to find comfort, to find a deeper understanding of something, and/or to connect with others, but we do *not* read to fill out a reading log or write a summary. Reading should be something students need to do and get to do to enhance their lives and the lives of others.

Here are a few examples of authentic responses to reading:

- Laughing out loud at a funny scene in a text
- Talking with a friend after reading something surprising
- Seeking out more information to read on a topic of interest
- Noticing an author's craft move and attempting to replicate it in their own writing

More on authentic response will be covered in Chapter 5.

Notes

How Do I Start to Build and Maintain a Reading Community?

WHAT IS A READING COMMUNITY?

A reading community is so much more than a group of students who read in class at the same time. A reading community is a thriving, ever-evolving group of different readers who come together to talk about books, reflect on their reading together, support each other, share stories and successes and areas to work on, and grow together.

Building a reading community is an ongoing process that takes time and deliberate effort. Your classroom reading community in August or September will feel very different than the community your students have grown into come springtime. To start thinking about building your classroom reading community, be sure to keep your beliefs about reading instruction (see Beliefs, p. 11) at the forefront of your work and follow these five key principles.

Five Key Principles to Building a Reading Community

A reading community . . .

1. Emphasizes reading as fundamental
2. Moves from teacher-driven to student-driven
3. Is based on trust and relationships
4. Shares common language and procedures
5. Supports each other in times of need and moments of celebration

---

READING AS FUNDAMENTAL

A community is based on shared experiences and common ground. The way to share reading experiences and build common ground is through books. Sharing your knowledge about children's literature and frequent, ongoing talk about books will create shared experiences and common ground for all of the readers in your class.

Terms to Know

Kidwatching: The continual act of observing children in the classroom with awe and responding based on what you see (Goodman & Owacki, 2002).

Gradual release of responsibility (GRR): The intentional shift from teacher-directed to student-independent action; more on this in Chapter 3.

Teacher to Student Agency Progression

	Full Teacher Agency	Heavy Teacher Agency, Light Student Agency	Light Teacher Agency, Heavy Student Agency	Full Student Agency
Book Choice	The teacher provides carefully curated browsing boxes at each table at the beginning of the school year to observe students choosing books.	As the teacher learns more about student reading preferences, she starts to introduce students to new book choices in the classroom library for them to explore. Eventually, the browsing boxes are removed.	The teacher gives specific whole-group lessons to the class on how to choose books. During independent reading time on the same day or after, the teacher provides individual and small-group coaching to students as needed.	Students take full ownership of book choices. When they feel they need a bit of support, they seek out their teacher or peers for a bit of guidance and coaching.
Book Talks	The teacher gives two to three book talks during morning meeting. Students watch and listen.	The teacher gives a book talk as a model and then invites students to give a book talk. As the first student begins his talk, the teacher coaches by asking questions and giving prompts to support the student in giving the talk.	The teacher invites students to give book talks during morning meeting and listens in as students offer their talks. Prompts are only given if absolutely necessary.	Students offer book talks to each other throughout the school day on their own without initiation from the teacher. This might happen as they're waiting to come inside the classroom, during independent reading time, or anytime students talk with each other.
Classroom Library	The teacher organizes and curates the collection in the classroom library.	The teacher seeks out student input about what's working and what's not in the classroom library. Students respond with suggestions for improvement.	Students start to request books for the library on their own without prompting from the teacher.	In addition to requesting books to add to the library, students start to organize the library by creating book baskets.

MOVES FROM TEACHER-DRIVEN TO STUDENT-DRIVEN ACTIONS

Reading communities may be established by the teacher, but through kidwatching and gradual release of responsibility (GRR), they are eventually driven and maintained by students. Consider the progression from full teacher agency to full student agency shown in Teacher to Student Agency Progression. Not all students will arrive at the level to achieve complete independent agency at the same time. Part of your work as a teacher is to notice who still needs support and who is ready to do the work on their own. Throughout the progression, notice how the students not only learn from and collaborate with the teacher, but they also do so with their peers as members of a classroom reading community.

TRUST AND RELATIONSHIPS

An effective community trusts and cares for each other. These are a few ways to build trust and demonstrate care:

- Make an effort to honor your students' identities through your book choices. Ask yourself if all of your students have seen themselves and their families in a class read aloud.
- Ask students questions about themselves and take the time to listen before jumping in to give instruction or next steps.
- Honor all student voices each day by providing ample opportunities for children to talk with each other.

COMMON LANGUAGE AND A SET OF PROCEDURES AND ROUTINES

A community functions through use of a shared language and a set of procedures and routines. Eventually, teacher language becomes student language if intentionally used and practiced over time. Procedures and routines also become familiar and comforting. For example, one comforting and familiar procedure might be routinely coming in every morning to read choice books. Another might be students bringing their reading baggies and folders to the meeting area at the start of every reading lesson. The familiar use of language and routines will become engrained as a comforting part of the community over time.

SUPPORT IN TIMES OF NEED AND MOMENTS OF CELEBRATION

Consistently noticing and celebrating small, incremental successes in the reading classroom also help build and maintain a positive reading community. Small successes might include students discovering a series they love or another sitting and reading for a certain amount of time without distraction. Additionally, a reading community also rallies around students in times of need or struggle.

Consider, for example, the power of community for a former student in my classroom. Denny struggled to view himself as a reader at the beginning of fifth grade. He frequently picked up books, flipped through pages, and then abandoned them without considering his own interests and needs in his choices. During one reading time in October, Denny became visibly flustered in trying to find a book.

Violet, another student in class, noticed and asked, *"Denny, would you like some help finding a book?"* Aaron heard this and decided to chime in, *"Denny, what have you tried to find a book? Maybe we can help you think of a different way."* The three students spent some time chatting while looking through the classroom library. Eventually, Denny walked back to his table with three books in hand. He spent the rest of reading time alternating between the books to decide which one to read. He was clearly engrossed. As the class was dismissed to walk out to lunch, Denny ran over to Violet and Aaron, *"I found it! I found my book!"* Violet put her hand on Denny's shoulder and responded, *"We knew you would."*

This exchange among Denny, Violet, and Aaron not only shows how a community of readers support one another in times of need and struggle, but it also shows how keeping books at the center, building trust, and having a shared language and set of procedures leverages students to be the drivers of the community. This exchange would not have happened unless all of those principles were in place.

Notes

How Can I Set Up Conditions to Foster Authentic Student Talk and Collaboration?

While reading appears to be a mostly individual activity, it is inherently social. The existence and rise of book clubs perfectly illustrates this point. Readers make meaning in their own minds but refine it through discussion with others. For example, students enjoy talking about what they're reading—sharing thoughts and personal connections, discussing plot events, and examining characters they wonder about. When students are provided opportunities to work together and collaborate around their reading, their motivation and engagement will likely grow.

WHAT IS STUDENT COLLABORATION?

Student collaboration is not about completing an assignment together or dividing up work to finish a task. It is about using talk to support each other in reading growth and to celebrate successes. In a first-grade classroom, for instance, this might look like partners reading and talking about a stack of books about caterpillars and butterflies to learn how to care for their upcoming temporary class pets. In a fifth-grade classroom, this might look like two readers discussing their personal reading goals for the week ahead and making plans to check in with each other.

Discussions about reading and books will take place for different reasons and at different times during the school day. Some talk will be planned and a part of lessons, small groups, and reading partnerships, while at other times talk will be more spontaneous. The when and where of it will be determined by students.

CLASSROOM PRACTICES THAT SUPPORT STUDENT TALK AND COLLABORATION

- **Give frequent book talks.** A book talk is a brief talk about a book with the purpose of introducing the book to others. I make it a practice to give a book talk a few mornings a week during our morning meeting in class. Book talks usually include the title, author, and just enough about a book to interest a reader without giving too much away. Eventually, students will take over the morning book talks.
- **Model casual talk.** If you want students to engage in meaningful talk around books, they need to know what that kind of talk sounds like. One way to illustrate this for students is to directly model it. You can chat about books and reading during transitions, while waiting in line, or during the short in-between moments in the classroom. Periodically discuss upcoming books, articles, or news you've read and share insights about your own reading life.
- **Encourage talk during independent reading time.** Think about the last time you read a part in a book that made you laugh out loud or read an online article that pushed your thinking about an important topic. How about the last time you finished a really great book? It is likely that you wanted to talk with a friend about what you just read. This is the same for students. Inviting

students to talk with quiet voices during independent reading time about what they're reading is valuable because it helps them develop a natural way to react and respond as engaged readers. You can even practice using quiet reading voices with the class so they become accustomed to the volume of talk that is required to make this work.

- **Student fishbowl.** Teacher modeling is powerful, but students modeling for each other can be much more so. In a fishbowl, two or more students sit in the middle of a large circle of other students. The students in the middle model a certain strategy. After teaching students some appropriate ways to talk about books, ask students to demonstrate some form of talk around their reading.

Amia and Sam model for the whole class how to talk with a friend about books.

- **Reading partnerships.** Consistent reading partnerships are a way to help students build ongoing collaboration and talk with the same partner over time. At the start of each new reading unit (or every 3–5 weeks), I recommend pairing students with a new partner. Partners can discuss many things: what they are reading, their thinking around their current reading, setting goals, checking in and giving updates on their goals, and offering words of encouragement that will push each other forward.

- **Book mingle.** A "book mingle" is a short (3–5 minute) activity in which students walk around the classroom to music with their current independent reading book in hand. In a kindergarten or first-grade classroom, students will choose their favorite book in their book box or bag to share. When the music stops, students stop to talk about their books with the person or people closest to them.

In the image on the left, music is playing and students move about the room. In the image on the right, the music has stopped, so Andrew and Tres are chatting about their books with each other.

- **Book clubs.** The purpose of book clubs is for students to have a shared experience through reading. While students might read their book club books on their own, the heart of the club is found in the talk that students engage in around the book. Sometimes, book club talk is structured to follow a supportive format. Other times, book club talk is free-flowing and more spontaneous. More on book clubs will be discussed in Chapter 3 (see Book Clubs, p. 89).

- **Share, practice, and display conversation stems.** Sometimes, students know exactly what to say. Other times, they might need a bit of support. Introducing, practicing, and then displaying a list of conversation sentence stems to support talk around reading will provide that bit of extra support that some students might need at different times. Here are some common conversation stems:

  - I think _____ because _____.

  - I wonder why _____.

  - I agree because _____.

  - I respectfully disagree because _____.

  - Tell me more about _____.

WHAT WILL STUDENTS TALK ABOUT?

Consider starting the school year with a lesson about how to talk about books. In this lesson, you and your students will generate different ideas for what you might talk about around reading. The two charts pictured here were generated with students in a first-grade classroom and a fifth-grade classroom. The charts hang in the classrooms all year and are updated or revised periodically as students learn more.

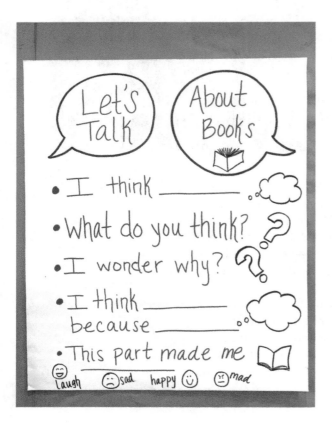

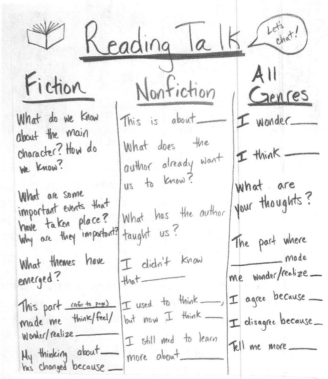

How Do I Involve Families and Caregivers in Their Child's Reading Life?

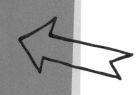

WHAT ROLE DO FAMILIES AND CAREGIVERS PLAY IN A STUDENT'S READING LIFE?

The role of families and caregivers in a student's reading life involves more than overseeing home reading and viewing report cards. It's an important balance to both communicate and engage with families without requiring them to do more than what is practical and meaningful in their lives.

Early in the school year, I encourage families to figure out how at-home reading will work for them. These are some ideas for you to consider sharing with them:

- Families finding time to read books or other forms of text together as often as possible. Daily is ideal, but it's important to honor and respect that some families can't make that happen due to work schedules or other valuable commitments.
- Reading in a family's home language other than English should be encouraged. Let your classroom families know that students reading in their home language also supports their growth in reading English (Bialystok, 2006; Chin & Wigglesworth, 2007).
- Setting up a system for students to bring books and other reading material back and forth from home each day will make it more likely that students will read at home. Simply put, reading will not take place if there isn't any reading material available.
- There are many different, valuable ways to include reading in home life:
  - Listening to audiobooks in the car or while helping with household responsibilities
  - Reading to a sibling
  - Reading a book or article online
  - Reading a recipe online and then cooking together

Reading lives outside of school look different for different students—just like the reading lives of adults look different. Families and caregivers will want and need to know what your expectations are for their child's reading outside of school. After all, they are the ones who will support students in this yearlong effort outside of your classroom. Over the years, I have reframed the way I view and communicate at-home reading expectations with students and families.

Equity

Assuming that every child and family can make the time for 45 uninterrupted minutes of reading each night is both unrealistic and inequitable. Rather than requiring what families do at home, include them in the process by asking them what might make sense in their busy lives and schedules.

Communicating About Reading Outside of School	
Instead of This	**Try This**
Referring to reading outside of school as "homework"	Refer to reading outside of school as "building your personal reading habit." If you call it homework, it means it's being done as a requirement for the teacher; if it's referred to as a personal habit, students are positioned to make their own choices and decisions.
Calling it "reading at home" or "before-bed reading"	Call it "personal reading" or "reading away from school." For many of your students, reading outside of school might not take place at home or before bed. Some students read in an after-school program, while on the bus home, or even while waiting at a sibling's sports practice. Invite students to think about the best place and time of day for them to read outside of school. This will likely be different for all students.
Requiring a certain number of minutes for reading	Support students and caregivers in identifying reasonable and meaningful times to read. Very few readers outside of school set a timer for themselves to read for 20, 30, or even 40 minutes. It's more likely that a person will sit down to read the next chapter or two in a novel, listen to an audiobook while they are taking their dog for a walk, or search for an informative article to learn something new. Finding authentic ways and sensible times to support students and families with fitting reading into their home lives will go a lot farther than requiring a specific number of minutes to read.
Telling students what to read	Invite students to choose their own reading material—books, magazines, comic books, and even audiobooks are all valuable formats for reading. Time away from school should be about students exploring their own interests and figuring out how to make authentic reading a part of their lives. Support students in doing this by encouraging them to make their own decisions about reading away from school.
Assigning a reading log and caregiver signature	Confer with students about their reading lives outside of school. Ask them what is working, what is not, and if they can make small adjustments to help themselves. Let parents know that you trust your students to read when the time is right for them, so a reading log is not part of your reading instruction. Rather, you are interested in supporting students in building a reading habit of their own design that fits in with their lives outside of school.

When you reframe the way you think about at-home reading, not only are you putting your students in control of their own reading lives, but you are also sending the message to families that you respect their time and their lives at home.

COMMON QUESTIONS AND CONCERNS FROM FAMILIES AND CAREGIVERS

Over my 20 years of teaching, I have found that some of the same questions and concerns repeatedly arise from families and caregivers about their child's reading away from school, including these:

- Is it OK that my child reads the same books over and over?
- How can I challenge my child in reading?
- My child only reads graphic novels and comics.
- My child doesn't like to read.

Answers are not always clear, and communicating big ideas about reading can be tricky. Always remember, all families and caregivers want the best for their children. Helping families and caregivers find the right answers will likely include more than one conversation or presentation. Appendix F offers tips and talking points to address some of these common questions and concerns.

Keep in Mind

For many teachers, Back to School Night or Curriculum Night in the fall is often the first opportunity to engage with families and caregivers. Take time on this occasion to let families and caregivers know that you appreciate them and respect their lives at home. Share both your views of reading outside of school and your core beliefs about reading.

Notes

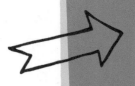

How Can I Continually Work to Make My Teaching Culturally and Linguistically Relevant?

The work of making your instruction, materials, and environment culturally and linguistically relevant is a careerlong endeavor. Your actions and decisions will change every school year, based on the students in your reading community. Every decision you make in the classroom will be informed by the cultural and linguistic identities of your students. From the books you choose for guided reading lessons to the actions you take to invite students' home languages into your classroom, culturally and linguistically relevant teaching is woven into every part of your day.

The suggestions in this section just scratch the surface of the important body of work that can inform your thinking, planning, and practice. With each recommendation comes a suggestion for further reading from expert scholars and teachers in the field. Infuse these principles throughout your teaching to truly keep students at the center.

Five Key Principles for Culturally and Linguistically Relevant Teaching

1. Get to know yourself and your students.
2. Critically examine texts.
3. Provide an intellectually stimulating environment for all.
4. Honor all languages.
5. Center joy.

GET TO KNOW YOURSELF AND STUDENTS

You cannot work toward being a culturally and linguistically responsive teacher unless you take the time to examine your own identity and biases first. A good starting point for this work is a resource called Test Yourself for Hidden Bias from the *Learning for Justice* website (www.learningforjustice.org). This is continual work that never stops. I embarked on this self-examination of my own identity and biases in 2017, and I am still deeply engrossed in learning about how my identity and biases play a role in my teaching. It is a lifelong endeavor.

Keep in Mind

Some parts of your own identity or your students' identities may feel uncomfortable to share. Only share what you are comfortable with and invite your students to do the same.

After starting a deeper self-examination, your next step is to honestly share your own identity with students. Students cannot be expected to share their identities with you if you are not open with them. Then, take the time to get to know and honor all the pieces that make up their unique identities. One way to approach this is through identity webs. Identity webs are a tool for students and teachers to make visible and celebrate their identities in the classroom. Once you begin doing this, you can start your work as a responsive teacher. To learn more on identity webs, check out *Being the Change: Lessons and Strategies to Teach Social Comprehension* by Sara K. Ahmed (2018).

CRITICALLY EXAMINE THE TEXTS YOU HAVE AND THE TEXTS YOU DON'T

A major part of working toward being a culturally responsive teacher is ensuring that *all* of your students see themselves throughout your classroom library and in your read alouds. It is also critical that you make sure your students see others. In her groundbreaking 1990 essay "Mirrors, Windows, and Sliding Glass Doors", Dr. Rudine Sims Bishop wrote, "When children cannot find themselves reflected in the books they read, or when the images they see are distorted, negative, or laughable, they learn a powerful lesson about how they are devalued in the society of which they are a part" (p. 13). To make sure all students—and all people—are valued in classrooms, teachers must make an effort to represent all classroom cultures and languages in their classroom libraries and read alouds.

Additionally, just because a book is written for children does not mean it is appropriate to have in your classroom. Some children's books, especially those that share an incomplete or biased view of history or groups of people, need to be removed.

Equity

When deciding whether to keep or weed a book, be sure to examine both the text and the images for biases and harmful stereotypes.

WORK TO PROVIDE AN INTELLECTUALLY STIMULATING LEARNING EXPERIENCE FOR ALL

Studies have found that students of color and those who are learning English as an additional language (English language learners, or ELLs) are frequently given less intellectually stimulating work in school than their white peers (Darling-Hammond, 2001; Oakes, 2005). All students have the right to schoolwork and reading that invites them to think critically. Many schools are so wrapped up in a culture of back-to-basics intervention that they are neglecting the intellectual strengths and needs of their students of color and ELLs.

While I recommend working toward changing the system over the long term, there are also steps you can take in your own classroom to combat this "pedagogy of poverty" (Haberman, 1991). Zaretta Hammond lays out a framework for teachers in her book, *Culturally Responsive Teaching and the Brain: Promoting Authentic Engagement and Rigor Among Culturally and Linguistically Diverse Students* (2015). Two key elements in Hammond's framework include shifting the student–teacher relationship to a learning partnership and working to create a socially safe environment for learning. Both ideas play integral roles in building and maintaining a thriving reading community.

HONOR ALL STUDENT LANGUAGES

Your students' home languages are a valuable part of their identities. When you invite and include the languages of your students into your classroom, you send the message that each language is a valuable and honored asset in your learning community. Including books in the classroom library and inviting students to write and share stories in their home languages are ways to work toward this. Consider also using translanguaging strategies in the classroom. Dr. Carla España and Dr. Luz Herrera describe translanguaging as when "a multilingual person's full linguistic repertoire is used and honored, instead of trying to keep narrowly focused on a single language" (2020, p. 21).

CENTER JOY

Dr. Gholdy Muhammad (2020) shares that a central lesson from Black literary societies was that literacy was directly tied to joy and love. Our children desperately need more joy and love in schools today! This is an idea that will take a little daily effort in your planning. Teaching history ethically and honestly is important and desperately needed. However, for every story of social injustice that you share in your classroom, share five that center on kids living joyful lives every day! This is especially important with the books that you share through read alouds and include in your library.

Great Resources

Getting to Know Yourself and Students

- *Learning for Justice* website, Test Yourself for Hidden Bias: https://www.learningforjustice.org/professional-development/test-yourself-for-hidden-bias

- *Being the Change* by Sara K. Ahmed (Heinemann, 2018)

Critically Examining Texts (Blogs)

- *American Indians in Children's Literature (AICL)*, Dr. Debbie Reese and Dr. Jean Mendoza https://americanindiansinchildrensliterature.blogspot.com/

- *BookToss* from Dr. Laura Jiménez https://booktoss.org/

- *CrazyQuiltEdi* from Edith Campbell https://crazyquiltedi.blog/

Providing an Intellectually Stimulating Experience for All

- *Cultivating Genius* by Gholdy Muhammad (Scholastic, 2020)

- *Culturally Responsive Teaching and the Brain* by Zaretta Hammond (Corwin, 2015)

Translanguaging

- *En Comunidad* by Carla España and Luz Herrera (Heinemann, 2020)

chapter TWO

HOW DO I STRUCTURE, ORGANIZE, AND PLAN MY READING INSTRUCTION?

Mr. Jackson, a first-year teacher just out of his credentialing program, felt a bit overwhelmed when thinking about how to organize and plan his instruction. Questions constantly swirled in his mind.

> Should I plan to focus more on fiction or nonfiction reading?
> What should I teach first to start off the school year? What next?
> Will all of my students enter my classroom already reading?
> How do I support students who might need extra help?
> How do I start to build a classroom library?

While Mr. Jackson felt prepared to teach actual lessons, he wasn't sure how to start planning and organizing his instruction.

Structuring, planning, and organizing instruction can be a rather challenging endeavor for many teachers. You will find more comfort with these things over time; however, before you can start to plan and organize your instruction, it is important to review or better understand the habits and skills required for proficient reading. It is likely that not all necessary reading habits and skills are included in your grade-level standards. For example, I have yet to read a standard that states, "*Students will learn how to consistently find books that they enjoy reading,*" yet that is one of the most important skills of proficient reading. Many factors play a role in successful structuring, planning, and organizing of reading instruction—it's no wonder early-career teachers and even many veteran teachers find it a bit daunting!

This chapter will answer all the questions that teachers have about how to structure, organize, and plan for reading instruction. It offers ideas for planning with a focus on flexibility and following the lead of the readers in class. The big ideas of equity, identity, and responsiveness will be woven throughout.

Twelve of Your Biggest Questions About How to Structure, Organize, and Plan Your Reading Instruction

Structure

1. What are the habits of engaged and joyful readers?

2. What are the skills of proficient reading?

3. What are some things to keep in mind about the similarities and differences in fiction and nonfiction reading?

4. What should a reading-centered classroom look and sound like?

Organize

5. How do I build and organize a classroom library?

6. How do I support students in choosing books?

7. How will I organize my classroom time to ensure students are reading enough?

8. What materials will students need, and how will they be stored?

Plan

9. How do I plan the scope and sequence of what to teach for the year?

10. How will I know what to teach next?

11. How can I plan to support students with specialized learning plans?

12. How can I plan to support all of the different needs of the readers in my class?

What Are the Habits of Engaged and Joyful Readers?

When thinking about planning for instruction, it is important to first think about the habits of engaged, joyful readers. When readers are engaged and finding joy in what they are reading, they are more likely to be open and receptive to learning the skills and strategies of proficient reading. Also, they are more likely to practice those skills and strategies over and over again because they will want to read. The more students read, the more they can practice the skills and strategies of good reading. The following five habits are goals for every reader to work toward over time. The more you model, explain, offer specific feedback, and provide time for practice with these habits, the more your students will grow into them over time.

FIVE HABITS OF ENGAGED AND JOYFUL READERS

Habit #1

Engaged and joyful readers sustain reading for a long period of uninterrupted time. In a kindergarten classroom, this may look like spending a solid 15 minutes with a stack of books without seeking out another activity. In a fifth-grade classroom, this might look like 45 minutes of being completely engrossed in a novel.

Habit #2

Engaged and joyful readers always have a book on deck. Engaged and joyful readers know that they will always need a book to read next. Not only will they keep a mental or written list of books to be read, but also they will know which one they want to read after the current one they are reading. In a kindergarten classroom, this might look like a book stack or basket on a child's desk to read in order of preference. In a fifth-grade classroom, this might be a written list of books to be read, often referred to as a "TBR" list.

Habit #3

Engaged and joyful readers are ritualistic about their reading. They might read in the same place at school or snuggle up in the same cozy corner at home to enjoy a book. They will often refer to these places as their "spot." They will also have preferred times to read outside of school. You might hear them say things like "I'm a before-bed reader" or "I always read right when I get home from school before I play video games."

Habit #4

Engaged and joyful readers read in the in-between moments, the moments of waiting and boredom that may arise throughout the day. Donalyn Miller refers to this as "stealing reading moments" (Miller, 2009). They do not need to wait for a sustained 20- to 45-minute uninterrupted period to read. Rather, they will always have a book with them so they can read while waiting in line or at the doctor's office. They might read while stuck at a sibling's sports practice or while waiting for dinner.

Habit #5

Engaged and joyful readers know that reading slumps are normal and temporary. They may fall into reading slumps every now and again when they can't seem to get into a book or find something engaging to read. Engaged and joyful readers know that this is just part of being a reader. It is not a sign things have gone sour in their reading lives, but rather it is something to work through.

TIPS FOR TEACHING THE HABITS OF ENGAGED AND JOYFUL READERS

Directly teaching the habits of engaged and joyful reading at the beginning of the school year and then periodically throughout the entire year will both support students in building these habits and save you valuable teaching time in the long run as fewer redirection and classroom management issues will arise.

I recommend kicking off the school year with a short lesson you design where you and the class co-create a list of things engaged and joyful readers do and how they do them. The ideas can be captured on chart paper and referred to again and again as needed. Pictured here are the charts from this lesson with a first-grade and fifth-grade class.

Great Resource

The Book Whisperer: Awakening the Inner Reader in Every Child by Donalyn Miller (Jossey-Bass, 2009)

What Are the Skills of Proficient Reading?

Proficient reading is defined as having a set of skills that enable a reader to read texts with accuracy and fluency to make meaning. These skills will grow the more time readers spend reading and as the texts they read increase in complexity. Many of these skills will be taught repeatedly by introducing readers to different strategies and providing them time to continually practice these strategies. The five big skills listed are the umbrella skills that cover hundreds of more specific skills. For example, comprehension is a big umbrella skill covering the more specific skill of identifying character growth over the course of a fictional story.

FIVE BIG SKILLS OF PROFICIENT READING

Skill #1 Comprehension

Proficient readers read to make meaning. They know every time they sit down to read, regardless of purpose, that they do so to make meaning and come to some sort of understanding.

Skill #2 Decoding and Word Recognition

Proficient readers work to figure out unknown or unfamiliar words. If they come across a word they do not know, they use all that they know to try to figure out the word. Decoding and word recognition instruction typically begin with phonemic awareness and phonics.

Skill #3 Fluency

Proficient readers read with fluency. Fluency is described as reading at a decent rate, plus reading with expression. This can be thought of as reading out loud sounding like a person's typical verbal speech. Reading fluently opens up cognitive space for meaning making.

Skill #4 Self-Monitoring

Proficient readers self-monitor while they are reading. They make attempts to correct mistakes at the word level, reread to make sure their reading sounds right, and are consistently monitoring for their own understanding. They also monitor for when they have lost focus or need to make a physical/mental adjustment in order to continue reading.

Skill #5 | Response and Reflection

Proficient readers respond to their reading in personal, authentic ways. This may be as small as coming to an opinion, such as thinking, "I loved that poem" or "That book wasn't for me," to as big as writing to a congressperson based on reading a news article or seeking out more books from the same author after becoming engrossed in a text.

LEARNING THE SPECIFIC SKILLS FOR YOUR GRADE LEVEL

Learning the different skills that you might need to teach at the different grade levels goes well beyond the scope of this book. Understanding the standards or learning targets for your grade level is important. Most states have their standards posted online for easy reference. Additionally, you will have students in your classroom whose zone of proximal development (Vygotsky, 1978) for some skills will fall outside of your grade level. Once you are familiar with your grade level's reading standards for learning, it is also important to become familiar with the standards in grade levels both above and below your specific grade in which you likely will need to support some students. Then, turning to multiple trusted evidence- and research-based resources will support you in this work.

Terms to Know

Zone of proximal development (ZPD): A theory of learning and development from Lev Vygotsky. The ZPD refers to the learning area that resides just above what a student is able to do independently. In a student's ZPD, they are ready to take on new skills and work with coaching and support.

Text levels: Irene Fountas and Gay Su Pinnell (F&P) created a gradient of text levels to guide teachers in assessing readers and choosing texts specifically for guided reading instruction (see Guided Reading, p. 88). The A to Z levels include descriptors for the different text features and reading skills and behaviors needed to fully decode and comprehend a particular text. Their intention with the text-level gradient is to level books, not to label children. The F&P Text Level Gradient™ is one of many different text leveling systems. All text levels mentioned in this book are F&P levels. Text levels do not always neatly align with grade levels. Correlation charts for text levels with different systems can be found with a simple online search.

LEARNING THE STAGES OF READING DEVELOPMENT

To better understand some of the skills you will need to teach your readers, it helps to have a basic understanding of the stages of reading development. The Five Stages of Reading Development chart shows just a few of the many skills students are learning and practicing throughout the five stages of reading development.

STRUCTURE

The Five Stages of Reading Development					
	Emergent	**Early**	**Transitional**	**Early Fluent**	**Fluent**
Text levels	aa–C	D–J	K–M	N–P	Q+
*Grade levels	K–1	K–2	1–3	2–5	3–5
Some text features	-Often repetitive -Often decodable -Pictures also tell the story	-One-, two-, and three-syllable words -More complex stories/ information -Pictures still often tell the story	-Multiple genres and series books -Longer and more complex sentences -More new vocabulary	-Multiple themes present -More complex characters or information -More complex sentence structures and vocabulary	-More complex characters, themes, and storylines -Information may include multiple main ideas
Some skills students will learn	-Recognize high-frequency words -Sustain reading rate -Tell what is happening	-Read simple multisyllabic words -Practice inflection when reading -Retell story/ information -Share opinion	-Read in longer phrases -Solve for new vocabulary through decoding and context -Predict and summarize	-Automaticity when reading most words -Predicting, summarizing, and inferring	-All prior listed skills plus deeper analysis and more complex comprehension skills

Chart informed by *The Fountas and Pinnell Continuum of Literacy Learning* (Heinemann, 2017).

Grade-level ranges are approximate. Readers at every developmental stage can be found throughout the grade levels.

Great Resources

Consult your school's curriculum. Additionally, the following books will support you in this work:

- *The Continuum of Literacy Learning* by Irene Fountas and Gay Su Pinnell (Heinemann, 2017)
- *The Reading Strategies Book* by Jennifer Serravalo (Heinemann, 2015)

Notes

What Are Some Things to Keep in Mind About the Similarities and Differences in Fiction and Nonfiction Reading?

There is an old notion that you likely have heard: Primary grade students *learn to read,* mostly with fiction, while intermediate grade students *read to learn,* mostly with nonfiction. In a 2021 podcast interview, Dr. Nell Duke explains that this statement, while possibly well intended, is actually a misinterpretation of the work of Dr. Jeanne Chall from the 1960s (Loftus & Sappington, 2021). In fact, all elementary readers are concurrently learning to read and reading to learn; it is not an either/ or endeavor.

It is important for teachers of reading to understand how nonfiction and fiction reading are similar and different. In some respects, the reading strategies and skills students learn can be applied to both genres. In other ways, there are key differences to understand.

Different Types of Fiction and Nonfiction	
Fiction: Story that tells about imaginary events and characters	**Nonfiction: A writer's telling of factual topics, events, and people**
• Realistic • Historical • Fantasy • Science fiction • Mystery • Adventure	• Biography, autobiography • Memoir • Narrative • Expository • History • Journalism • Instructional, procedural

Keep in Mind

Formats Versus Genres: Formats and genres are often confused. All genres can be written in multiple formats. These are some common formats:

- Poetry
- Prose
- Graphic
- Comic

FIVE BIG IDEAS FOR UNDERSTANDING FICTION

- Fiction is largely based on plots, which unfold through characters' words, actions, interactions, and events.
- Characters often grow and change throughout a fictional story.

- Most fiction in elementary reading follows an arc of a story introduction (learning the setting and meeting the main characters), events leading to a problem, a problem, and finally a resolution to the problem. Arcs in fiction become more complex as students' reading material increases in complexity.
- Fiction books need to be read from the first page to the last in their entirety either in one sitting or over time.
- Most fiction has a theme. A theme is a big recurring idea or message. As texts become more complex, multiple themes will be woven throughout. Often in primary grade fiction, themes will be explicitly stated. As books become more complex, students will likely need to infer or draw conclusions to determine the theme, as it is not explicitly stated. Sometimes, the theme is referred to as the moral or the author's message, but the correct instructional term is "theme."

FIVE BIG IDEAS FOR UNDERSTANDING NONFICTION

- Rather than telling students that reading nonfiction is about reading the truth, it is wise to tell students that reading nonfiction is about reading a writer's version or understanding of the truth. This is especially important in the upper grades as students start to read more historical accounts of the past and current events.
- Most nonfiction focuses on one topic, but multiple structures can be found throughout each text. Some common structures include chronological, cause and effect, and how-to.
- Nonfiction often has a main idea that is supported by examples and evidence. As books grow more complex, multiple main ideas will be present.
- Nonfiction is often, but not always, comprised of text features throughout. Some of these text features include photographs, captions, charts, maps, cutaway images, and more. Text features help boost understanding of more complex material.
- Nonfiction does not necessarily need to be read from the first page to the final page, especially expository nonfiction. Students need to learn how to use text structure and common nonfiction text features in order to understand how to navigate a nonfiction text.

BALANCING THE TEACHING OF FICTION AND NONFICTION

Different recommendations abound for exactly how much fiction or nonfiction teachers should use in their reading instruction. A good rule of thumb is to make sure to have a good balance of nonfiction and fiction reading in your classroom. Many elementary teachers follow an approximate 50/50 model—half of their reading instruction is with fiction, while the other half is with nonfiction. Students need instruction in both.

Notes

What Should a Reading-Centered Classroom Look and Sound Like?

In a reading-centered classroom, a visitor will see students reading! This reading might take place independently, in partnerships, in groups or clubs, and at centers or learning stations. They might also see the teacher conferring with students, teaching a small group, or even reading a book aloud to the entire class. The classroom library will be a focal point of the classroom. Baskets of books arranged by author, genre, and topic will be present. Reading notebooks, book bags or boxes, and comfortable spaces to read will also be present. Very rarely will a reading-centered classroom be silent. The sounds of students talking, pages turning, and teacher instruction will fill the air.

ON THE WALLS

Rather than store-bought charts, the walls of a reading-centered classroom may feature instructional charts co-created during lessons, student writing about reading, and student book recommendations. It's important that the items on the walls reflect your students' learning needs and reading identities too. Charts that you co-create with students are often the most effective because these help transfer learning.

THE LAYOUT

The layout of a reading-centered room will provide many spaces for students to comfortably settle into reading and for the teacher to provide instruction in small groups. The classroom will likely include a large meeting area, where whole-group instruction and read alouds will take place, and a large circular or horseshoe-shaped table for small-group instruction. In primary classrooms, there will likely be breakout spaces for students to work in reading-focused stations.

Reading-centered classrooms will typically include a classroom library, a meeting area for students to gather for lessons and read alouds, cozy spots to read, work stations, and a small-group table.

Take a Tour of a Reading-Centered Classroom

Scan the QR codes to see a tour of a reading-centered first-grade and fifth-grade classroom (above and below, respectively).

resources.corwin.com/answerselementaryreading

To read a QR code, you must have a smartphone or tablet with a camera. We recommend that you download a QR code reader app that is made specifically for your phone or tablet brand.

STRUCTURE

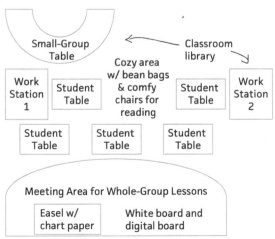

What Should a Reading-Centered Classroom Look and Sound Like?

45

How Do I Build and Organize a Classroom Library?

The classroom library is the cornerstone of every reading classroom. It should be an organized, inviting space where students feel like they see themselves and each other. Books should be coming and going frequently. Books are meant to be read and passed from reader to reader, not protected and stashed away from students. Sounds of previewing books of flipping pages and phrases such as "This book made me think of you" should be common sounds in the classroom library throughout the school day.

Keep in Mind

Using a classroom library may be a new adventure for some students. Together with your class, create a list of ways to use and maintain the library. Keep the list posted in your library. Here are a couple of list items to get you started:

- Look for books you'll enjoy reading.
- Work together to keep the library organized.

In elementary classroom libraries, books are typically arranged in bins, facing forward for easy student browsing access. Sections of the library might be organized by genre, topic, or author. These are decisions you can make based on your students' interests—ask them to help you organize the library!

Sometimes, teachers choose to liven up the library with plants, lamps, and even cozy seating.

Portions of a first-grade library and a fifth-grade classroom library

TIPS FOR *GROWING* A CLASSROOM LIBRARY

Great Resources 🔍

Grants for Books

- Book Love Foundation: www.booklovefoundation.org
- Donors Choose: www.donorschoose.org
- First Book: www.firstbook.org

Tip 1

As a starting point, consider the students you teach in choosing books for the library. Ask yourself if their identities, interests, and preferences are represented in the library.

Tip 2

To keep on top of what is current in children's literature, consult book blogs that are continually updated. Appendix E includes a list of websites and book blogs to follow.

Tip 3

Ask students what they would like to see included in the library. Each time I ask my students to recommend books for the library, they offer suggestions that are new to me.

Tip 4

Make use of the Scholastic Book Club. Their bonus points system is a gift to classroom libraries everywhere! Over the years, I have acquired many free books this way. Additionally, grants for classroom and school libraries can provide needed funding.

Tip 5

Seek out help. Classroom libraries are often underfunded, and many teachers feel pressure to supply books themselves. That can be overwhelming and unaffordable! Ask your principal, school librarian, and other staff about ways to gain funding for your classroom library to keep it relevant and growing. There are many ways to acquire current, relevant books for your classroom library without breaking your budget. Also, you and your grade-level team might consider rotating book collections through your classrooms. Doing this provides book access to more readers.

TIPS FOR *ORGANIZING* THE CLASSROOM LIBRARY

Tip 1

For ease in student browsing, place books in bins labeled by topic, series, and author. Eventually, invite students to create book bins. Some student-created book bins in my classroom have included the labels *Stories About Friendship*, *If You Liked Wings of Fire, Try____,* and *Laugh Out Loud (LOL)*.

Tip 2

Avoid labeling books as gendered or diverse. "Girls' books" and "boys' books" are not categories; in fact, books with these labels do not exist. Additionally, when books are labeled as diverse and separated into their own bin, they are being *othered*, or labeled as different from the accepted norm. This is a harmful practice that must be avoided.

Tip 3

To keep the library fresh and engaging, periodically rotate book bins in and out. When rotating a new book bin into the classroom library, be sure to introduce it to the whole class. While the books might not be new, these additions will be new to your library from your students' perspectives, and that in itself is very exciting for young readers!

Tip 4

Make a *Book Return* box. When students are unsure of where to return a book, they can place it in the Book Return box. This will prevent books from being misplaced in the library.

Tip 5

Don't be afraid to weed out books, especially books that are in bad shape, unread, and problematic. Remove books that have not been touched in years. It can be difficult for readers to find books if they have to sift through lots and lots of old, uninteresting titles in order to find a gem. Also, some books' images perpetuate harmful stereotypes or even inaccurate textual information. These books have no place in classroom libraries. For more information on this, I recommend reading Dr. Laura Jiménez's blog *BookToss* (www.booktoss.org) and following her on Twitter.

Classroom Library Book Return Box

How Do I Support Students in Choosing Books?

After searching for a book for 5 minutes in the classroom library, Annie read the back of *Esperanza Rising* by Pam Muñoz Ryan and decided to take it back to her desk to read. Her teacher's initial response was to intervene, as *Esperanza Rising* was labeled as a few levels above Annie's current independent reading level. But when she saw Annie settle in to comfortably read, she decided to allow her to keep going and to check in on her progress in the book the next day.

Supporting students in choosing books plays a key role in planning for instruction. Sometimes—as in planning guided reading lessons, for instance—you will choose books for students. However, students should be choosing most of their reading material themselves. When you simply hand a student a book to read or keep them from reading certain parts of the classroom library, you may inadvertently send a message that you do not trust them to make their own choices or that they are not capable of making their own choices. Also, choice does not mean lack of foundation or structure. When we teach students how to choose books for themselves, they develop tools they will continually use for life both inside and outside of the classroom.

BOOK CHOICE IS VITAL TO AGENTIVE READING

Choosing books is a vital reading skill that needs to be taught and revisited over time. It is perhaps the most important skill in which readers should feel comfortable and confident; it is the skill that will keep them reading. If students are not choosing books on their own, they likely are not reading on their own either when the teacher isn't present.

There are many strategies that can be used to choose books; I'll cover a few later in this section. Students who are not yet comfortable with choosing books on their own need to know and practice many of these strategies to become skilled with book choice. However, choosing books is truly an imperfect practice. Embrace the imperfection and messiness of it! Adult readers even make missteps when choosing books for themselves. We often abandon books when they are not appealing. Becoming skilled in book choice is a long process. There is no end point.

SKILLED BOOK CHOICE OVER READING LEVEL

Skilled book choice involves the intersection of interest and readability, or books that students *want* to read and *can* read. Rather than simply viewing readability as a text level or level based on a computerized program, I recommend taking on a more comprehensive approach. Many factors play a role in readability: background knowledge, vocabulary, interest, text density, and more. Students who have background knowledge and an invested interest in a book's topic can likely independently read books above what is considered their current independent reading level. Plus, when you teach students how to choose reading materials for themselves, you can coach them on ways to determine whether the text itself will cause frustration, and you can offer solutions for working through challenging texts.

Keep in Mind

Fountas and Pinnell have stated that levels are a tool for teachers to inform instructional decisions, such as with guided reading. They are not a means for students to choose books or for teachers to label students. All students deserve to choose their own books!

Remember Annie? When her teacher sat down with her to confer about her choice of *Esperanza Rising* the next day, Annie told her teacher she learned of a connection with Esperanza and her own family. "Esperanza's family is like my mom's family. My mom has told me stories about growing up that sounded kind of like Esperanza. Can I bring this book home to show her?" At that moment, Annie's teacher was so glad she had not intervened in Annie's book choice. Because Annie's background knowledge, familiarity with vocabulary, and motivation supported her understanding, *Esperanza Rising* was clearly a solid book choice for her, despite being labeled as above her independent reading level.

Keep in Mind

Myth: Offering students book choice is an unstructured free-for-all.

Reality: The strategies involved in the skill of choosing books need to be explicitly taught.

TEACHING STUDENTS HOW TO CHOOSE READING MATERIALS

Teaching book choice is not a one-size-fits-all endeavor. After teaching a couple of whole-group lessons on book choice, observe your students as they make their book choices. Determine who needs more teacher support and who might need a bit of light support. Once you've determined what your students need, try some of the following methods and conferring language to provide that support.

Methods and Language for Teaching and Supporting Book Choice

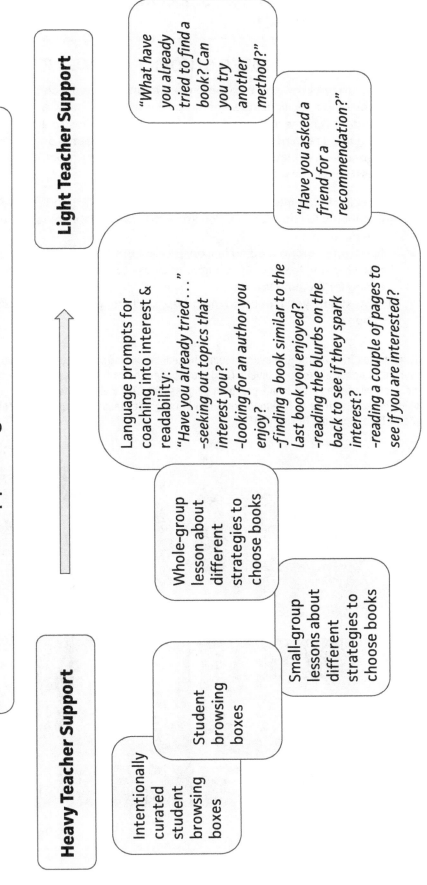

Light Teacher Support

"What have you already tried to find a book? Can you try another method?"

"Have you asked a friend for a recommendation?"

Language prompts for coaching into interest & readability:

"Have you already tried . . . "
-seeking out topics that interest you?
-looking for an author you enjoy?
-finding a book similar to the last book you enjoyed?
-reading the blurbs on the back to see if they spark interest?
-reading a couple of pages to see if you are interested?

Whole-group lesson about different strategies to choose books

Small-group lessons about different strategies to choose books

Student browsing boxes

Intentionally curated student browsing boxes

Heavy Teacher Support

BOOK CHOICE METHODS: FROM HEAVY TO LIGHT TEACHER SUPPORT

INTENTIONALLY CURATED STUDENT BROWSING BOXES

Intentionally curated browsing boxes are used to offer students choice in books while still providing specific texts selected by the teacher. One way these are used is to offer students choice in books at their independent or instructional reading level after a guided reading lesson. Doing this ensures students are reading books at their independent or instructional level in addition to other books they choose from the classroom library. Here's how it works:

1 You collect high-interest books at a particular level or band of levels for students to choose from. You know the levels of the texts, but the students do not.
2 After a small-group reading lesson, present the box of books to students. Invite students to choose a number of books to include in their book bags for reading for the next few days.
3 The next time you meet with the group, students will be able to swap out books.

Browsing boxes from a first-grade classroom: The teacher intentionally curated these boxes to include books at certain reading levels. Only the teacher knows the levels and will offer students choice in certain boxes after small-group reading lessons. More about intentionally curated browsing boxes specifically for kindergarten and first-grade classrooms will be explained in Chapter 3 (see Browsing Boxes, p. 100).

STUDENT BROWSING BOXES

Student browsing boxes are similar to intentionally curated browsing boxes. The only difference is that the books in student browsing boxes are not necessarily leveled or selected based on specific criteria aside from student engagement. At the start of the school year, I place lots of different books in boxes for students to choose from before the classroom library is open. A box is placed at each student table for browsing until the library is open a few days later. Doing this helps me see which books students are drawn to and even which books are missing. Students will always let me know which books they'd like to read if they are not in the box!

WHOLE-GROUP AND SMALL-GROUP BOOK CHOICE LESSONS

Much of the language used for individually coaching students in how to choose books can also be used in whole-group and small-group lessons. The skill you are teaching is choosing books students *can* read and *want to* read. There are many strategies that students can use to work toward that skill. The charts seen here were created with students in a second-grade class and fifth-grade class during whole-group book choice lessons. Teaching book choice in kindergarten and first grade is a bit different. More on that will be explained in Chapter 3 (see Books, p. 98).

STRUCTURE

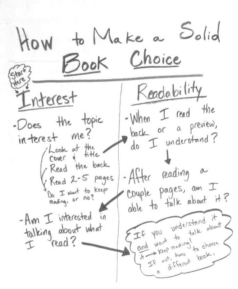

> *Steps to Teaching a Small- or Whole-Group Book Choice Lesson*
>
> 1. Prepare: Gather a few books from your classroom library to model how to gauge a book for interest and readability. Make sure you have chart paper and pens ready.
>
> 2. Gather students in the classroom meeting area.
>
> 3. Discuss a few methods for finding good books to read with your students (see a few of the language prompts or Book Choice charts for ideas). Also, invite students to share their ideas. Capture the shared book-finding strategies on your chart paper.
>
> 4. Model how to gauge a few books for interest and readability.
>
> 5. Invite students to practice looking for books based on interest and readability. They may search in the classroom library or in browsing boxes.

COACHING INTO INTEREST AND READABILITY

Individually coaching students during conferences is another effective way to support book choice. Using the language prompts listed in the Methods and Language for Teaching and Supporting Book Choice chart is a great starting place. The big idea to keep in mind with this is that you want to avoid making book choices for students. Rather, you want to hand over the agency to your students through coaching. If you simply give a book to students who are having trouble choosing, they will possibly read that one book and then likely have trouble choosing their next book. If you take time to coach those same students in how they can support themselves in choosing a book, they will likely build strategies over time for how to pick books on their own.

Notes

How Will I Organize My Classroom Time to Ensure Students Are Reading Enough?

Ms. Singh's class engages in literacy work at different points throughout the entire school day. They start their day with a fun read aloud, then move into literacy-based stations. In these stations, her students engage in word work, writing, and teacher-led small-group reading. At another point in the day, she leads her class in a shared reading lesson with a poem and then an interactive read aloud. However, due to all her literacy time being highly teacher directed, Ms. Singh can't shake the feeling that despite all of the rich literacy work her students engage in, they don't seem to have enough independent reading time.

"Reading volume" is the term used to refer to how much time students spend reading, plus the number of words read (Allington, 2012). Teachers base whether students are reading enough on their reading volume. Multiple studies over the years have shown the benefits of a high reading volume (Allen et al., 2015; Allington, 2012; Anderson et al., 1988; McVee et al., 2005; Ozuru et al., 2009). Not only does reading volume play a role in engagement, but it also plays a key role in students' supported practice of all the habits, skills, and strategies you've taught to help them continually grow. Without ample time for reading in school, students will not be able to engage in the reading practice that they need to progress. Plus, they will likely not find engagement in reading if they do not get to do it frequently. You can't control or make assumptions about your students' reading practices at home, so providing ample time to read during the school day is key.

> Students Reading Independently
>
> + Teacher Instruction in Conferences, Small Groups, and Stations
>
> = Supported Independent Reading

Reading volume is not exactly easy to measure. Some measures, such as home reading logs, are not always accurate and can also decrease reading motivation (Pak & Weseley, 2012), which lessens volume. The best way to ensure your students are reading enough is to organize your instructional time to provide supported independent reading every school day without exception. If possible, organize your schedule to provide more than one period of supported independent reading. So in addition to using assessment to gauge how your students are doing (see Chapter 4 for more on assessment), it is also important to self-assess how you organize your instructional time to make room for independent reading (see Chapter 3 for more on instructional decision-making).

Consider the following kindergarten and fifth-grade schedules. Notice how each teacher breaks up supported independent reading time (shown in bold in the schedule) to fit in different places throughout the day. Also, students have an opportunity to practice reading throughout their entire school day. Students encounter reading opportunities all throughout the day in social studies, science, writing, and even in math! How might you fit in supported independent reading time throughout your school day?

Keep in Mind

It takes consistent practice over an extended period of time to build stamina for reading. One way to support students in building reading stamina is to increase reading time in small increments each week until you reach your desired amount of time in class. You can even graph the time you read with your class to celebrate every increase in time!

Kindergarten Schedule	
8:00–8:20	Morning Circle Time
8:20–8:30	**Free Choice Reading Time**
8:30–9:10	Interactive Read Aloud
9:10–9:30	Phonemic Awareness and Phonics
9:30–9:45	Recess Playtime
9:45–10:00	Shared Reading on a Social Studies or Science Topic
10:00–10:10	Reading Lesson
10:10–10:45	**Reading Stations**
10:45–11:00	Movement Break
11:00–11:45	Math Lesson and Stations
11:45–12:25	Lunch and Playtime
12:25–1:00	Writing Workshop
1:00–1:15	**Relaxing Reading Time**
1:15–1:30	Closing Circle Time

Fifth-Grade Schedule	
8:00–8:20	**Morning Choice Reading Soft Start**
8:20–8:35	Morning Meeting
8:35–10:00	Math
10:00–10:20	Recess
10:20–10:45	Interactive Read Aloud
10:45–11:45	Writing Workshop
11:45–12:25	Lunch
12:25–1:25	**Reading Lesson and Supported Independent Reading**
1:25–2:25	Science, Social Studies, PE, or Art
2:25–2:35	Closing Circle Time

Notes

What Materials Will Students Need, and How Will They Be Stored?

Years ago, I taught a student, Ryan, who was a self-proclaimed airplane enthusiast. He loved everything about airplanes and the idea of flying. Ryan loved airplanes so much that on his birthday that year his family drove to a field near San Francisco International Airport for a picnic so he could watch the planes take off and land.

In addition to being a self-proclaimed airplane enthusiast, Ryan was a self-proclaimed "hater of reading." These were his words. This is how much he disliked reading. I tried every strategy I knew to help Ryan enjoy reading. And, honestly, nothing worked. All of the children's and middle-grade books on the topic of airplanes did not seem to interest him.

When I chatted with his mom to learn more information, she let me know that the only time she ever saw Ryan deeply engaged in his reading was when they were on an airplane and he was reading the in-flight magazine. So ever since then, she tried to collect in-flight magazines from any airline she could.

I knew that it didn't matter what Ryan read; it just mattered that he did, in fact, read! So I sent messages to all of my friends and family near and far and asked them to collect and send me the in-flight magazines when they traveled by airplane. Each time I was able to bring in a new in-flight magazine for Ryan, he was both joyful and deeply engaged in reading!

Above all else, students need reading material. It is important that classroom libraries are stocked with lots of different books (see p. 47), but there are also other materials that will be needed by both you and your students for reading instruction.

Keep in Mind

Supplying your classroom with needed materials is not about getting the latest book or the fancy sticky notes. It's about gathering the materials that will get your students excited about reading!

Common Materials in the Reading Classroom		
	What Is It?	**Why Is It Important?**
Independent reading material	Books Comic books Graphic texts Magazines Audiobooks Digital and online texts	The act of reading takes many different forms. As long as students can make meaning from it, it is a worthy form of text.
Book bag or box	A container to house reading material. In K–2 classrooms, alphabet charts and other tools may be included to support reading.	It provides easy, predictable access to reading material and supports students in staying organized.

(Continued)

What Materials Will Students Need, and How Will They Be Stored?

57

(Continued)

Common Materials in the Reading Classroom		
	What Is It?	**Why Is It Important?**
Reading mat	A place to organize book stacks for reading, typically in kindergarten and first-grade classrooms.	A reading mat supports K–1 readers in reading all of the books in their book box and then starting again once they finish.
Reading folder	A place to keep reminders from lessons and other tools for reading, such as alphabet charts.	Students need a place to access reminders of their learning.
Reading notebook	Third- through fifth-grade readers can keep a reading notebook to jot down their thoughts/sketches about their reading and important reminders and notes from reading lessons.	Reading notebooks are a place for upper-grade students to keep a record of their thinking while reading. Throughout the school year, students can refer to their thinking about the books they read. With a reading notebook, they can see how much they have grown as readers over time and even write down goals they are working on and goals they have met.
Sticky notes	A place for teachers to leave reminders of learning for students and for students to jot notes and thinking about their reading.	Sometimes, it's important for teachers to jot a quick reminder of learning to leave with students. Other times, it's important for students to capture their thinking in the form of a quick note to leave in their books while they are reading.

Reading mats can be found in many primary classrooms. To use a reading mat, students place all of their books in the order of preference on one side of the mat. As each book is read, it is placed on the other side of the mat. Once all books are read, students move the books back to the other side of the mat to keep reading.

Reading notebooks are a common tool for students in upper-grade classrooms to capture their thinking around their reading. This is a page from Fiona's reading notebook, showing her thinking while she was reading a nonfiction book about wolves.

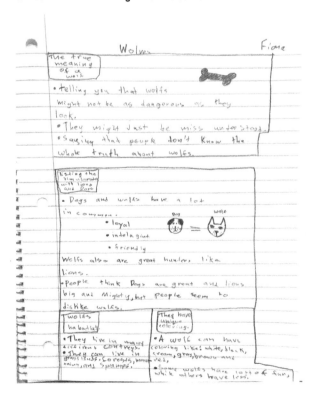

What Materials Will Students Need, and How Will They Be Stored?

59

How Do I Plan the Scope and Sequence of What to Teach for the Year?

It is likely your school follows a certain curricular calendar or a scope and sequence of units to teach throughout the school year. The scope refers to what is taught, while the sequence refers to the order in which the skills and strategies in each unit and the units themselves are taught. Most curriculums follow a genre-based sequence. If your school does not follow a particular curriculum or scope and sequence, the planning will be determined by you and the other teachers on your staff. If you do not have a curriculum or scope and sequence to follow, you will want to reach out to your teaching colleagues to start planning together.

HOW LONG SHOULD I SPEND IN EACH UNIT?

Typically, a reading curricular unit should last between three and five weeks. This provides enough time to teach the important pieces of a unit while still holding the interest of students. Within a school year, it is important for all students to experience lessons and units in foundational reading skills, fiction, and nonfiction reading.

WHEN SHOULD I FOCUS ON READING HABITS?

In addition to kicking off a school year with lessons on building reading habits, it is recommended to intersperse reading habit lessons throughout the year. It's always a good idea to build in a whole-group lesson on a reading habit if you feel your class will benefit. For example, a reading habit lesson I revisit a few times each school year is centered around *what to do when it's hard to focus on reading*. Follow the lead of your students. By continually kidwatching (more on this in Chapter 4), you will learn what your students need.

HOW DO FOUNDATIONAL READING SKILLS FIT IN?

Critical reading foundational skills are interspersed all year long in every genre-based unit through lessons, group work, shared reading, interactive read alouds, and within the other components of balanced literacy. Units are typically genre-based rather than skills-based, as the skills of proficient reading are needed to read every genre. For example, if you teach first grade, during a fiction reading unit you might plan to include some whole-group lessons on new phonics patterns, daily shared reading with poems to incorporate phonological awareness, a station focused on a familiar phonics game, and small strategy groups to teach decoding of the CVC and CVCe spelling patterns (C = consonant, V = vowel, e = silent e). This is just one way you might incorporate foundational skills into a genre-based unit. There are many other ways as well. The key is to always inform your decision-making with what you see your students need. More on this will be explained in Chapter 4 on formative assessment.

WHAT ABOUT POETRY?

Poetry should not be saved for the month of April when we recognize National Poetry Month. It should also be woven throughout the school year. Some teachers have adopted a practice called Poetry Fridays, where they share a new poem every Friday with their class. Another way to incorporate poetry is through shared reading each week with a new poem or putting a poem on the board a few mornings a week for students to read and discuss in morning meeting.

HOW FAR IN ADVANCE SHOULD I PLAN?

A good first step in planning is to sit down and spend time figuring out in which order you will teach your units for the school year. Oftentimes, this is work that grade-level teams do together. Then, about a week or so before each new unit is to start, plan out the scope and sequence of individual lessons and interactive read alouds. These will be your big anchors in guiding the rest of your planning with the other components of balanced literacy throughout your weeks. Your daily and weekly planning of small groups, reading stations, and conferences within each unit should be based on the immediate needs of your students through formative assessment and planned on a week-by-week and sometimes even day-by-day basis. Plans should always be written in pencil, as it is likely they will change based on the needs of your students.

This is a Weekly Instructional Reading Plan from Ms. Cohen's classroom. Notice where she wrote TBD (to be determined) in the schedule. Ms. Cohen typically plans lessons only a few days ahead, as she knows her students' needs for learning may change. A blank instructional plan can be found in Appendix G.

Weekly Reading Instructional Plan

Dates 10/4 - 10/9   Current Reading Unit _Understanding Information_

Whole Group Lessons	
Monday	Finding and exploring nonfiction texts that are interesting.
Tuesday	Previewing a nonfiction text using images, captions, subheading.
Wednesday	Identifying main idea and supports
Thursday	↓ ↓ ↓
Friday	Monitoring for making sense

Read Alouds	Interactive	For Enjoyment or Other Reason
Monday	If Sharks Disappeared by Lily Williams	I am Every Good Thing by Derrick Barnes
Tuesday	Main Idea & Supports	We Are Water Protectors by Carole Lindstorm
Wednesday	Seashells More Than A Home by Melissa Stewart	(TBD)
Thursday	Determining Importance	———
Friday		(TBD)

Stations This Week	Partner Read	Word Study	———

Small Groups	Students	Instructional Focus
Monday	Meg, Raj, Joey, Elsa	Solving Unknown Words
	Tamar, Angel, Andre, Lila, Omar	Determining Importance
	Celia, Midori, Stephen, Theo	Book Choice
Tuesday	Meg, Raj, Joey, Elsa	Monitoring for Sense
	Vivi, Carson, Marc, Anna, Lin, Lavar	Creating Personal Goals
Wednesday	Tamar, Andre, Lila, Omar, Angel	(TBD based on Mon.)
	Reva, Harrison, Kayleigh, Evan, Deeann	Determining Importance
Thursday	Meg, Raj, Joey Elsa	(TBD based on Tues.)
	Celia, Midori, Stephen Theo	(TBD based on Mon & Tues)
Friday	Meg, Raj, Joey, Elsa	(TBD based on Thurs)

Reading Conferences	
Monday	Joey, Reva, Deeann
Tuesday	Celia, Midori, Stephen, Theo
Wednesday	Meg, Raj, Joey, Elsa, Midori
Thursday	Tamar, Angel, Vivi, Carson, Marc
Friday	Joey, Andre, Lila, Omar, Anna, Lin, Lavar

STRUCTURE

How Will I Know What to Teach Next?

🔑

Equity

Following a curriculum page by page is not equitable. True equity is working to follow the lead of your readers by asking what they need and then adjusting plans accordingly.

When planning for instruction, the number-one key principle is to always follow the lead of the readers in front of you. Many teachers are required to follow a curriculum or a sequence of standards. However, within your planning it is critical that the students in front of you are considered before anything else.

Generally following a sequence of lessons is a good idea, but be sure to do so flexibly rather than rigidly. Always leave room for formative assessment to guide your decision-making for what to teach next.

FORMATIVE VERSUS SUMMATIVE ASSESSMENT

Formative assessments are the assessments that you do every single day to inform your teaching. Some forms of formative assessments in reading include sitting with children to listen to them read, engaging in a casual conversation about a book, and stepping back and watching the entire class during independent reading or center time. Every time you base teaching decisions on what you directly see or learn that your students need, you are engaging in formative assessment. It is a good idea to keep notes on your formative assessments. More on this is discussed in Chapter 4.

Summative assessments are typically school district or state mandated. These are the assessments that do not immediately inform your teaching. Oftentimes, the results of summative assessments are not available until weeks or even months after the assessment was given. Examples of this include standardized tests given each spring.

FORMATIVE ASSESSMENT GUIDING TEACHING

Formative assessments will let you know what you should teach next. Sometimes, your assessments will reveal that you can move on to the next lesson in your plans without making adjustments. Often, your assessments will reveal that a handful of students still need practice with a certain concept. In this case, you might choose to pull a small group and still move forward in the sequence of your planned lessons. Other times, you might find that more than half of the students are not making progress with a taught concept. This shows that you need to consider reteaching the concept in a different way—or reevaluate the concept being taught altogether.

A NOTE ABOUT PROGRESS AND MASTERY IN FORMATIVE ASSESSMENT

When you plan lessons and make decisions about what to teach next, first decide if students are expected to show progress or mastery. Typically, it takes multiple exposures and a lot of practice for a concept to be mastered. It is important not to expect mastery when first teaching a concept, but rather to expect and celebrate progress. For example, if you are teaching students how to identify details that support the main idea in a nonfiction text, it is important to understand that students will need initial direct instruction, ample time to practice in their own texts, and often support from you provided in small groups and conferences over a period of time before they reach mastery. Mastery should not be expected after the initial lesson!

The chart seen below can be used as a guide for what to teach next, based on what formative assessment shows.

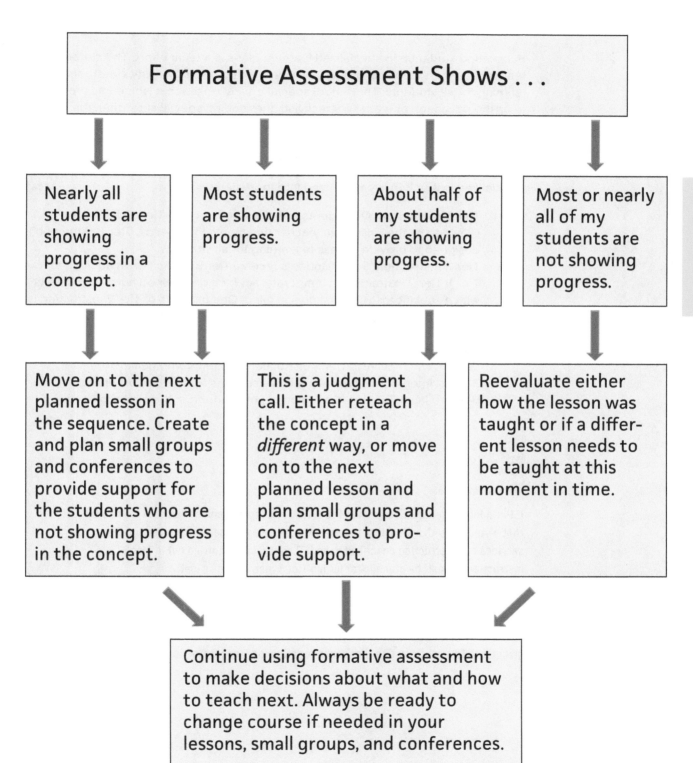

How Can I Plan to Support Students With Specialized Learning Plans?

Supporting students on specialized learning plans is a team effort. The classroom teacher is always involved and plays a key role in providing quality classroom learning for all students. The school special education teacher (sometimes referred to as the education or learning specialist), the reading specialist teacher, the school psychologist, the speech pathologist, various other specialists (such as occupational therapist or school social worker), and the school principal all may play roles in contributing to and implementing specialized learning plans as well.

Specialized instruction is categorized into three tiers:

- **Tier 1 instruction**: All students in a classroom receive Tier 1 instruction provided by the classroom teacher that meets their needs. Tier 1 instruction is designed to provide access to learning for all students.
- **Tier 2 instruction**: Some students receive Tier 2 instruction in addition to Tier 1. Tier 2 instruction is temporary, set for a determined number of weeks with a specific instructional goal in mind. One example of Tier 2 instruction is a student meeting with the reading specialist teacher for six weeks to reach a specific academic goal.
- **Tier 3 instruction**: The most intensive level of individualized instruction a student can receive is Tier 3 instruction. Students who qualify for a Tier 3–level intervention typically receive services from a support provider detailed in an IEP plan in addition to your support in the classroom.

Terms to Know

IEP: An Individualized Educational Plan (IEP) is a legal document written to ensure that a student with a disability receives specialized services and instruction. The services and instruction described in an IEP are typically carried out in Tier 3 instruction but will be planned for within Tier 1 instruction as well.

504 plan: A 504 plan is a legal document written to ensure that a student with a medical diagnosis or disability receives accommodations and modifications in the classroom in order to access learning. An example of a 504 plan accommodation is giving a child a seat close to the teacher or allowing frequent movement breaks.

CLASSROOM TEACHING IMPLICATIONS

- A common misunderstanding is that the classroom teacher does not play a role in specialized services for students. In fact, the classroom teacher always plays a key role. Whether it be ensuring a student has access to a particular audiobook, collaborating with a specialist to refine Tier 1 instruction, or checking in frequently with caregivers, the classroom teacher is always the first provider of instruction for students on a specialized plan.

- Collaboration and inclusion are the keys to successfully implementing specialized learning plans in the classroom. Students who receive services based on a learning plan should always feel included and valued in the classroom. To make this happen, the classroom teacher will closely collaborate with specialized staff, caregivers, and the student to ensure success.

Notes

STRUCTURE

How Can I Plan to Support All of the Different Needs of the Readers in My Class?

All students in your classroom will have different needs as readers at different times. Following the strengths and needs of readers as your primary guide will support your work in providing them what they need.

Five Key Principles of Supporting All Readers

1. Consider both access and differentiation.
2. Make frequent use of formative assessment.
3. Strategically use scaffolds.
4. Seek support from other teachers and staff.
5. If one method or strategy isn't working, try another.

CONSIDER BOTH ACCESS AND DIFFERENTIATION

Access is offered to the whole class while differentiation is offered to a few. If you offer access for all students before differentiation, you are providing necessary supports in order to learn without singling out a student. An example of this might be taking the whole class outside for a 3-minute movement break instead of asking a paraprofessional to take one or two students outside who appear to need a break. Some strategies like this work well for the whole class. Others require specific differentiation.

Terms to Know

Productive struggle: The opportunity for students to grapple with new learning within their zone of proximal development.

MAKING THE MOST OF FORMATIVE ASSESSMENT

Determine what readers can do before providing additional support. Avoid the urge to jump in to help right away. Sometimes, all that's required is asking a question or two and a little bit of wait time. This allows students to feel and build more agency for their own learning. At the point of difficulty or struggle, ask questions to support problem-solving and engagement with productive struggle instead of telling them how to solve a problem (Burkins & Yaris, 2016).

- What methods have you tried to help yourself?
- What else can you try to help yourself?
- How do you know that worked?

By starting with questions like these instead of problem-solving for a student, you will be positioned to see what your student can already do before you decide how to provide support. Oftentimes, some teachers tend to provide more help than what is needed. By taking the time to assess what students can do first, you are building their agency and opening up your teaching time to introduce new learning. All students, especially those learning English as an additional language, deserve to engage in productive struggle that will help them grow and flourish as readers (Hammond, 2015). We cannot support students in productive struggle unless we determine what it is they can do first on their own through formative assessment.

PLANNING THE USE OF SCAFFOLDS

A scaffold is a temporary support that is used in order to complete a task. A scaffold should never become a permanent crutch for students. When providing a student with a scaffold, it is important to have a clear plan to remove it.

For example, providing a student with a bookmark to place below lines of text they are reading to help their eyes stay on track and then return sweep down to the next line is a temporary scaffold. Eventually, students who use this scaffold will not need to use it once their eyes track without the support. Through consistent kidwatching and use of formative assessment (see Chapter 4), you will decide when your student no longer needs a scaffold.

SEEK SUPPORT FROM OTHER TEACHERS AND STAFF

My former principal, Mary Pat O'Connell, coined a motto for the staff at my school that we still firmly grasp onto even though she is now retired: *We all teach all the children.* This motto has led my staff to lean on each other and turn to each other when any of us need advice or help in supporting a student. Seeking support or help is a sign that you care about providing for your students' strengths and needs. Never worry about asking for help. When in doubt, *always* ask.

HOW WILL I KNOW WHEN TO TRY A NEW STRATEGY?

If a lesson did not stick with students or they are having a difficult time with something, more practice might be needed. If more practice does not seem to help, teach the concept or idea in a different way. Keep in mind that teaching the same thing over again the exact same way will likely produce the same results. If you're looking for different results, try teaching or explaining in a different way. Also remember to reach out for help! You likely have colleagues with vast experience to tap into.

Great Resources

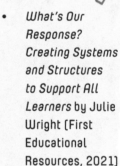

- *What's Our Response? Creating Systems and Structures to Support All Learners* by Julie Wright (First Educational Resources, 2021)

- *Culturally Responsive Teaching and the Brain* by Zaretta Hammond (Corwin, 2015)

- *Good to Great Teaching: Focusing on Literacy Work That Matters* by Mary Howard (Heinemann, 2012)

chapter THREE

WHAT ARE THE KEY INSTRUCTIONAL PRINCIPLES TO KNOW AND USE?

Ms. Valencia, a veteran eighth-grade English teacher, needed a change. She decided to put her K–8 teaching credential to use and switch grade levels—to second grade! While she's incredibly well versed in supporting the needs and strengths of a group of eighth-grade readers, she hasn't taught elementary school in over 15 years. Among many of the questions running through her mind, she wondered if her instruction should focus on whole-group lessons or more on small-group work. She also worried about what all the other students would be doing when she works with a student one-on-one. This chapter will answer Ms. Valencia's questions and more about some of the specifics of how to balance and conduct all of the aspects of reading instruction in an elementary classroom.

Throughout the six-year grade span in elementary schools, common components of instruction will be found within each of the grade levels. For example, interactive read alouds, short and clear lessons, and teacher-supported independent reading time will be present in every grade level. Because of the unique nature of teaching reading to 5-, 6-, and 7-year-olds, the final question in this chapter is devoted to some special aspects and considerations of teaching kindergarten and first-grade reading.

This chapter introduces many instructional concepts and practices that should be explored in more depth. Each question in the chapter suggests resources for further learning. When you're ready, I recommend taking a deeper dive into one of the topics that piques your interest or is of greatest need in your community of readers.

Ten of Your Biggest Questions About the Key Instructional Principles to Know and Use

1. What are the different choices and models I have for instruction?

2. What are the different components of balanced literacy in reading instruction?

3. How should I balance whole-group instruction with small-group and individualized instruction?

4. How do I deliver a lesson to the whole class?

5. How do I make the most of an interactive read aloud?

6. How do I make the most of student independent reading time?

7. What are some different structures for small-group learning?

8. How does a reading conference go?

9. How can I incorporate reading throughout the entire school day?

10. What are some special considerations in the K–1 classroom?

What Are the Different Choices and Models I Have for Instruction?

There are a variety of ways teachers can ensure students have access to the **Five Key Principles of Reading Instruction:**

1. Direct instruction of reading skills, strategies, and concepts
2. Opportunity for inquiry—to ask questions, explore, and discover learning on their own or in collaboration with others
3. Ample time for reading practice after direct instruction or inquiry
4. Individual feedback from the teacher to adjust and refine learning
5. Opportunity to reflect on their learning

The instructional models that are proven by research and classroom practice to be highly effective are balanced literacy, the gradual release of responsibility, and the workshop model. All of these can work together, too, as you'll read in the following sections. I encourage you to check out the books listed here for a deeper look at these crucial models for instruction.

BALANCED LITERACY

Balanced literacy, although recently challenged for not including enough direct instruction in phonemic awareness and phonics in some cases, is a model that is widely and successfully used in many schools. Michael Pressley, an educational psychologist, coined the term in his book *Reading Instruction That Works: The Case for Balanced Teaching* (1998). Subsequent editions of the book, co-written with literacy education scholar Richard Allington, have shared revised thinking of balanced literacy.

While many definitions of balanced literacy have been bounced around the education realm since 1998, Fisher et al. (2020, p. 3) provide a reasoned and thorough description in *This Is Balanced Literacy*. Balanced literacy is *"maintaining equilibrium across language arts domains (reading, writing, speaking, listening, and viewing), ensuring students have access to instruction in foundational skills (phonemic awareness, phonics, fluency) and meaning making (vocabulary and comprehension), and varying instructional delivery modes (direct, dialogic, and independent)."*

Balanced literacy is comprised of different components that are strategically used at different times for different purposes (details on the components can be found in the next question in this chapter). Reading is taught by implementing the different components in a variety of ways. In some elementary classrooms, reading is taught in one large block, typically ranging from 90 minutes to two hours. In other classrooms, the different components of balanced literacy instruction are taught at different times of the day. The times and schedules you implement will vary based on your school, grade level, and classroom situation.

GRADUAL RELEASE OF RESPONSIBILITY

In the gradual release of responsibility (GRR) model (Pearson & Gallagher, 1983), the teacher offers direct instruction through modeling what students will ultimately do on their own. The GRR model is often referred to as the "I do, we do, you do" method of instruction.

- *I do*: The teacher clearly models what the students will practice so they can see and hear what they will do next.
- *We do*: The students practice what the teacher just modeled as the teacher actively coaches students during their work.
- *You do*: The students are invited to independently work on what they just practiced. The teacher observes as the students start to independently work in order to continue coaching students who need more support.

THE WORKSHOP MODEL

First conceptualized by Donald Graves and Donald Murray (1980) as a model for the teaching of writing, the workshop model is the most versatile and the most often misunderstood model of instruction in literacy education. The workshop model can take the form of the GRR model and can infuse all components of balanced literacy when intentionally implemented. Workshop consists of three parts:

1. A 7- to 15-minute lesson that directly teaches one concept, idea, or standard.
2. A 20- to 45-minute supported independent reading time where the teacher supports readers through intentionally planned small groups, conferences, and sometimes reading-focused stations based on formative assessment.
3. A 2- to 5-minute share period where students reflect on their learning.

Reading Workshop and Gradual Release of Responsibility at a Glance			
Length of Classroom Time	**Part of the Workshop Model**	**Part of the Gradual Release of Responsibility Model**	**Key Principles of Reading Instruction Addressed**
7–15 minutes	**Lesson delivery**	The "**I do**" part of teaching	**Principles 1 & 2** The teacher clearly explains and models what the students are learning to do and practice. At times, in lieu of directly explaining or modeling, the teacher can guide students through an inquiry for instruction.

(Continued)

What Are the Different Choices and Models I Have for Instruction?

71

(Continued)

	Reading Workshop and Gradual Release of Responsibility at a Glance		
Length of Classroom Time	**Part of the Workshop Model**	**Part of the Gradual Release of Responsibility Model**	**Key Principles of Reading Instruction Addressed**
20–45 minutes, depending on the lesson and grade level	**Supported independent reading time** with teacher-led small groups, conferences, and sometimes reading-focused stations the entire time.	Both "**we do**" and "**you do**" The "we do" part of the model happens with the teacher leading small groups and reading conferences. The "I do" part is students reading independently.	**Principles 2, 3, & 4** This is the independent and supported reading time for students. All students will be independently reading or working in reading-focused stations during this time while the teacher pulls small groups and holds one-to-one conferences to provide more individualized support.
2–5 minutes	**Reflection or sharing:** Students are given the opportunity to share their reading, thinking, or to independently reflect on their learning from the session.	Continuation of the "you do" part of learning.	**Principle 5** Students should always have the opportunity to think about and reflect on the reading work they do in class. This might include jotting down something they are proud of, making plans for tomorrow's reading based on today's, or even turning to talk with a friend about what they just read.

Great Resources

This Is Balanced Literacy by Doug Fisher, Nancy Frey, and Nancy Akhavan (Corwin, 2020)

A Guide to the Reading Workshop: Primary Grades by Lucy Calkins (Heinemann, 2015)

A Guide to the Reading Workshop: Intermediate Grades by Lucy Calkins (Heinemann, 2017)

PUTTING IT ALL TOGETHER

The beauty of balanced literacy, GRR, and workshop is that they all work together and can be implemented in conjunction with any curriculum or set of standards (more on how balanced literacy works in conjunction with GRR and workshop will be explained in the next section). At the same time, the core of all three is following the lead of the readers in front of you. Nothing is more important in the teaching of reading than following the lead of students and making instructional decisions based on your ongoing formative assessment.

What Are the Different Components of Balanced Literacy in Reading Instruction?

Part of the trickiness of a balanced literacy practice is finding the right balance each year for the students in front of you. No two years of teaching will ever strike the same balance, as all readers will come to your classroom with different strengths and needs. Use the strengths and needs of the readers in front of you to guide your decision-making.

Once you commit to following the lead of your readers, the next step is determining which methods to put in place in your classroom. The following components play integral roles in striking a balance that will serve the strengths and needs of all of your readers.

Whole-group lessons are delivered to the entire class each day in one short time frame. Oftentimes, whole-group lessons are based on a curriculum or set of adopted standards. These lessons usually range from 7 to 15 minutes in length where you will explain and model a new reading concept for students to practice (see Whole-Class Lessons, p. 78).

Foundational skills instruction is a needed part of reading instruction for kindergarten through second-grade students. Some readers in the upper grades will also need specific instruction in foundational skills (to be determined through formative assessment; see Chapter 4). The foundational skills of reading include listening comprehension, concepts of print, phonemic awareness, and phonics (see K–1 Classrooms, p. 96).

Interactive read aloud is the time of day when you gather students for a read aloud focused on a specific skill or strategy. While reading aloud, you stop at predetermined points to facilitate student interaction around the text and skill or strategy being taught (learn more in Read Alouds, p. 80). Maria Walther's book *The Ramped-Up Read Aloud* (2019) is a go-to for interactive read alouds centered on current, diverse children's books.

Reading aloud for pleasure is another critical part of reading instruction. This is the time when you and your students gather to share in the joyful experience of listening to a story together. I agree with Lester Laminack (2016) that "the first hurdle in the teaching of reading is to build the love of books and stories and information." Reading aloud for pleasure is the time you get to solely devote to a love of reading.

Shared reading takes place when all eyes in the classroom are on the same text. In the primary grades, this is often in the form of a big book or a poem written in large print on chart paper. In the upper grades, this may be an on-screen projected article or a copy of a short text in each student's hands in addition to the projected copy. Shared reading typically happens over the course of a few sessions during

What Are the Different Components of Balanced Literacy in Reading Instruction?

73

the week. In Session 1, you read just to hear the story or information all together. Subsequent sessions may focus on skills such as phonics instruction, vocabulary development, fluency, comprehension, and even deeper analysis. *Shake Up Shared Reading* (Walther, 2022) is a great resource full of read alouds and follow-up shared reading lessons.

Guided reading is a small-group instructional method where students individually read the same book at their instructional level in a group setting to receive specific instruction based on their reading in the moment.

Strategy group instruction takes place to teach a specific reading strategy to a small group based on prior formative assessment. In strategy groups, students learn a strategy modeled by you and then will practice this strategy with your coaching and support.

Book clubs are student-driven reading groups that take place periodically throughout a school year. Typically, students choose which book they will read from choices you curate. The purpose of book clubs is for a small group of students to read and discuss a common text. (See Small-Group Learning, p. 87, to learn more about guided reading, strategy groups, and book clubs.)

Supported independent reading is the daily practice where your students will read books of their choosing on their own, sometimes with partners, or in reading-focused stations. While students are reading, you are providing support through small groups and reading conferences. To learn more about making the most of supported independent reading, see Independent Reading, p. 83.

Word study has taken many forms over the years. The study of how words are put together, pronounced, and understood should be a playful, engaging experience for students. From phonemic awareness and phonics in the lower grades to learning about roots and affixes in the upper grades, this time of day encompasses all that is involved with decoding, spelling, and understanding words. To learn more about word study, check out *Word Study That Sticks* by Pam Koutrakos (2018).

All components of writing instruction are a key part of a balanced literacy classroom. In fact, they play a pivotal role in reading development. M. Colleen Cruz posits, "When writers of all ages write a lot, they become better readers because they have the inside scoop on the work writers do" (2019, p. xvii). I strongly agree. Each time children sit with a book, they are reading someone else's writing. This is also true each time you share a read aloud with the class; you are reading and sharing a model of well-constructed writing. Katie Wood Ray describes it as "reading is the writer's way of visiting another craftperson's 'gallery'" (1999, p. 13).

One of my favorite ways to connect reading and writing in class is to invite students to read and comment on each other's writing. I've done this activity with all grade levels, and the result is just magic! Student readers love reading and commenting on each other's work. Additionally, student writers love reading their peers' feedback!

This is just one example of how reading and writing in the classroom are inherently connected. Student writers and readers at all grade levels simply love reading and commenting on each other's work!

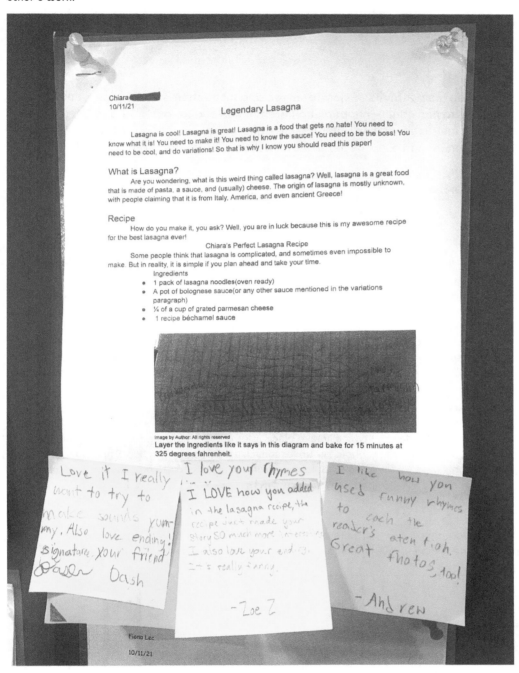

To learn more about writing instruction, see the companion book in this series on the teaching of writing by Melanie Meehan, *Answers to Your Biggest Questions About Teaching Elementary Writing* (2022). To learn more about tapping into the power of writing to teach reading, check out the *Writers Read Better* pair of books about nonfiction and narrative by M. Colleen Cruz (2018, 2019).

What Are the Different Components of Balanced Literacy in Reading Instruction?

75

How Should I Balance Whole-Group Instruction With Small-Group and Individualized Instruction?

The three main formats of classroom reading instruction—whole group, small group, and individual—happen at different times and for different purposes during reading instructional time. All three are equally important in our students' reading development and allow us to tailor instruction to students' strengths and needs.

	Whole Group	Small Group	Individual
Who receives this lesson?	The entire class	Usually three to five students	One student
Roughly how long is the typical lesson?	7–15 minutes	5–15 minutes, depending on the needs of each group	1 minute or less for quick check-ins; up to 7 minutes for in-depth conferences
Where does the lesson take place?	Typically, the teacher is at the front of the room and students are gathered in a meeting area near the teacher. Students may also be at their desks if spacing requirements are in place.	Most often, these lessons are given at a horseshoe-shaped or circular table. Sometimes, teachers choose to deliver small-group lessons in the meeting area on the floor at the front of the room.	The beauty of individual lessons, also known as conferring, is that they can be delivered anywhere in the classroom. Most often, they are given at the student's own desk or reading area.
When will these lessons take place?	Whole-group lessons in reading instruction are typically delivered once a day, sometimes more, at the start of reading instructional time.	Small-group lessons are a part of daily reading instruction that typically take place after the whole-group lesson. Usually, two to four small-group lessons are taught each day.	Like small-group lessons, individual reading conferences are a part of daily reading instruction. Three to five reading conferences are usually held each day. More can take place if the conferences are quick check-ins.
What is the rest of the class doing?	All students are together participating in the lesson.	The rest of the class is independently reading, doing partner reading, or working in reading-focused stations.	
What might it look like?			

Answers to Your Biggest Questions About Teaching Elementary Reading

HOW DO I KNOW WHICH FORMAT TO USE FOR WHICH LESSONS?

Whole-group lessons take place so teachers can deliver the specific grade-level standards or learning targets to the entire class of students at one time. Lessons outside of standards and learning targets should also be delivered to students if it is determined that more than roughly half of the class could benefit from the lesson. If it is determined that only a few students need the lesson, it is a better use of instructional time to forgo the whole-group lesson for a small-group lesson. It certainly won't hurt the whole class to receive the lesson, but it is not the best use of teaching minutes. Your valuable teaching minutes add up quickly!

 Equity

Ongoing small-group lessons and conferences are a key component of instructional equity, as they are the means for providing students specific instruction to meet their individual needs.

Small-group lessons serve the specific needs of a few students at one time. These lessons are powerful for three reasons:

1. They meet students' specific needs that might not be addressed in whole-group lessons.
2. They are a time-efficient way for a teacher to give targeted instruction to a few students at one time.
3. They offer students an opportunity to learn alongside and interact with other students in class under the guidance and coaching of the teacher.

A teacher will decide to group students for different reasons; there's more information on grouping later in this chapter. All small-group configurations are created to specifically meet students' common needs or strengths.

Individual lessons, also known as **conferring**, serve the specific needs of individual students. Individual conferences with students do not need to follow a specific formula, but they should follow some type of plan. Teachers can choose from many different types of conferences that meet students' needs and build on their strengths in different ways (see Question 8 of this chapter: *How does a reading conference go?*). Consider these two key guiding questions when sitting side by side to work with a student during a one-to-one conference:

1. What's going on with this reader right now?
2. How might I respond in the moment to move them forward? (Yates & Nosek, 2018)

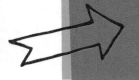

How Do I Deliver a Lesson to the Whole Class?

Ms. Ellenberger teaches a whole-group reading lesson in fifth grade.

Delivering a reading lesson to the whole class is an important part of every single day of reading instruction. Whole-class lessons typically teach new learning and are usually, but not always, based on a curriculum's scope and sequence. Regardless of which curriculum you might use, there are a few key principles that will make your whole-group reading lessons more effective.

Five Key Principles of Whole-Group Reading Lessons

1. Teach *one* learning target.
2. Model how to do it.
3. Engage students during the lesson.
4. Keep it short.
5. Provide time for practice right after the lesson.

Teach *one* learning target per lesson. It may be tempting to cover more than one standard or skill during a lesson. After all, there is a lot that needs to be taught within a school year. However, it is not an effective way to teach and would likely be too overwhelming for many students to learn. So it is important that you select one learning target that will benefit the whole group as the focus of each lesson.

Model how to do it so students know exactly what you are teaching and what they will soon be trying. The difference between a good lesson and a great lesson is that students walk away from a great lesson knowing exactly what to do next. One of the best ways to teach students what to do is to model it for them yourself. When thinking about the gradual release of responsibility (GRR) model (see GRR, p. 71), this is the "I do" portion of the lesson. Show students exactly how to do what it is you want them to do.

> One way to model a reading strategy is to use a big book, projected digital text, or a text under a document camera so all eyes are on the text while you are modeling using *thinking aloud,* which is sharing your thinking about what you are strategically doing as a reader. This makes your reading and thinking visible to students.

Engage students in trying out what you taught immediately after you model so it is fresh in their minds. Giving students the opportunity to try out what you just taught will not only give them immediate practice and opportunity for feedback in the moment, but it will also let you know right away if your students understood the lesson so you can make adjustments if necessary.

Keep it short! In elementary school, a whole-group reading lesson should be short so students can spend most of their time practicing what you just taught. Plus, it becomes very challenging for some students to sustain attention after 10 to 12 minutes of instruction. It's even difficult for many adults to sustain focus for that long!

Provide time for practice right after the lesson. To transfer what you just taught students to their own independent reading, it is important that they have ample time to practice right after the lesson (Wiggins, 2012). Students will not become proficient in the skills and strategies of good reading unless you provide them time to apply those skills and strategies in their own independent reading along with your support through small groups and conferences.

Keep in Mind

For each lesson, consider leaving a reminder of the learning for students by co-creating a chart during the lesson.

Notes

INSTRUCTION

How Do I Make the Most of an Interactive Read Aloud?

Without reservation, I can attest that read-aloud time is the most cherished time in my classroom—for all of us. It is the time when we all gather in our meeting area to be introduced to the life of a new character, to find out what is going on with an old friend, to learn a life lesson, or to learn something new. While this section focuses on interactive read alouds, which is an instructionally focused read aloud, I'd like to start with a simple yet powerful insight from Maria Walther, author of *Ramped Up Read Aloud* (2018): "First and foremost, a read aloud should be a joyful celebration for all" (p. 1).

While the interactive read aloud is a powerhouse instructional component of all reading classrooms, sometimes it is necessary to just gather your class to enjoy a book together—no lesson, no standards covered, just reading aloud for the sake of enjoying a book together. In the elementary teaching day, these two types of read alouds work together to support our readers: The read aloud for enjoyment supports our readers in growing a love of reading, in shaping who they are as readers. The interactive read aloud supports our readers in learning new skills, strategies, and even authors' crafts as readers and writers.

WHAT IS AN INTERACTIVE READ ALOUD?

An interactive read aloud is an instructional read aloud, typically done with a picture book, where students and the teacher are intentionally interacting with the text with a specific goal of learning in mind. While the teacher reads the text and discusses/shares the images in the text, students also interact with the text to increase their understanding of the skill being taught.

Five Ways Students Can Interact With the Text

Stop and Think	Stop and Jot a Note	Stop and Sketch	Turn and Talk With a Partner	Share Out to the Whole Group

WHEN SHOULD I DO AN INTERACTIVE READ ALOUD?

The interactive read aloud can be a stand-alone experience anytime during the school day. Alternatively, teachers can also use an interactive read aloud as the lesson to kick off independent reading time.

WHAT DOES AN INTERACTIVE READ ALOUD LOOK, SOUND, AND FEEL LIKE IN THE CLASSROOM?

Although it sounds simple, students get the most from an interactive read aloud that has been planned. Here's how to make the most of an interactive read-aloud experience, in planning and in action.

PLANNING FOR THE INTERACTIVE READ ALOUD

1 Based on a learning need you see in your classroom, select a learning target for your interactive read aloud.

2 Select a picture book that you love to read in which you will be able to guide students through the type of thinking that you determined in Step 1.

3 Read the book yourself one time through to appreciate the story and to know what to expect for your second read.

4 Re-read the book with your learning goal, target, or standard as a lens. Mark places to stop to invite students to think and add their ideas and thinking around the learning. The read aloud is truly interactive. You will be guiding students through interaction with the book focused on specific learning.

DOING THE INTERACTIVE READ ALOUD WITH STUDENTS

If you have time to devote two sessions to the read aloud, I recommend to first read the book to your students without stopping so students become familiar with the story. Upon their first read, the heavy cognitive lift will focus on understanding and enjoying the book. You can invite students to ask questions and share ideas before, during, and after the read aloud. The second read will focus on the learning that you planned and will typically take place in class the day after the first read.

1 Gather your students in the meeting area to engage in your casual first read of the book. Enjoy!

2 The next day, gather your students in the meeting area for your second read—the interactive read aloud of the same book.

3 Show your students the book and explain that you will be reading the book with a new focus.

4 Clearly state the new focus for your students. It may sound like this: *"Today, we are going to read _____ again. For this read, we are going to focus on _____."* It's helpful to read next to an easel with chart paper to write the lesson's focus and student learnings and ideas along the way.

5 Read the book based on the planning of Step 4, pausing in the places you've planned, asking questions, encouraging discussion, and jotting notes on the chart paper along the way.

6 Once the interactive read aloud is complete, remind students of what they learned and that they can apply this lesson in their own reading. *"We just learned how to _____. Don't forget, this is something you can always do when you read your own books."*

Equity

All students in your classroom need to see themselves represented in the read alouds you choose. See Appendix E for a list of recommendations for finding great books.

INSTRUCTION

After reading aloud a book with students, leave it on display for students to read during independent reading time. Seen here are read-aloud books displayed for student access from a first-grade and fifth-grade classroom.

Scan the code to watch how I plan an interactive read aloud.

Great Resources

Professional Books

Ramped Up Read Aloud by Maria Walther (Corwin, 2019)

Rebellious Read Alouds by Vera Ahiyya (Corwin, 2022)

Online Resources

Appendix E lists online resources for learning about and finding read-aloud books.

Notes

How Do I Make the Most of Student Independent Reading Time?

"Arguably, transfer is the aim of any education." —Grant Wiggins, 2012

To grow as readers, students must have ample time daily to read independently in a supported environment. This allows them to practice all the skills and strategies they have been taught so what they learn in reading lessons transfers to their independent reading. The only way for students to transfer what you teach to their own independent reading is by reading books and other forms of text every day in class with support. Nonreading activities around books may seem fun and worksheets may keep students occupied, but they do not support students in becoming proficient readers, nor do they support them in growing their love of reading. Frankly, these tasks are often a waste of instructional minutes. The only thing that supports students in reading is actual time spent reading with teacher support through small groups, stations, and conferences every single day, without exception.

Five Key Principles for a Successful Independent Reading Classroom Practice

1. Students should engage in supported independent reading every school day without exception.

2. Students should have access to a wide variety of culturally and linguistically relevant books representing different genres and topics for them to choose from that they can read and want to read.

3. Students should have ample time to independently read, from 10 to 25 minutes in the kindergarten classroom up to 35 to 50 minutes in the fifth-grade classroom.

4. Students should receive the support they need (classroom environment, well-stocked library, intentional lessons, small groups, stations, appropriate accommodations when necessary, and conferring after the lesson) to continue to grow while they are reading.

5. Students should have the opportunity to consistently share their reading and talk with classmates about their books.

WHAT DOES STUDENT INDEPENDENT READING TIME LOOK, SOUND, AND FEEL LIKE?

During independent reading time, all students are reading books of their choosing along with some texts potentially selected by the teacher. Some of the teacher-selected texts may include familiar guided reading books or texts within reading-focused stations. In all grade levels, the teacher is working with small groups and conferring while students are reading. However, there are some notable differences in each of the grade ranges. When students start in kindergarten, they will begin building their reading stamina with perhaps 5 to 10 minutes of supported independent reading to start. Incremental increases in time will continue through fifth grade, where students will sustain 30 to 45 minutes of supported independent reading in one sitting.

Supported Independent Reading Across Grade Levels			
Grades	What It Looks Like	What It Sounds Like	What It Feels Like
K–1	A visit to a kindergarten or first-grade reading classroom will show students scattered about the classroom reading independently, in partnerships, in groups under the guidance of the teacher, and spaced out at different learning stations. All students will have either a book bag or book box alongside them that houses their books and other reading materials.	Kindergarten and first-grade supported independent reading times will emit a beautiful noise! It's the noise of little voices reading many books to themselves and each other. Our youngest readers need to hear themselves, each other, and their teacher read. Teachers often practice reading voices with students at the onset of a school year. The result is a beautiful hum of readers reading!	The positive, playful energy that exudes from a kindergarten and first-grade independent reading time is unlike anything else!
2–3	In a second- and third-grade classroom during reading time, students will also read independently, with partners, and in groups with the teacher. In second grade, most students will likely have multiple shorter books they are reading at a time. A transition will start to take place for some in second grade and many in third grade. Some students will have multiple shorter books at once, while others are starting to settle into reading one longer book at a time.	Second- and third-grade supported independent reading time may not be as beautifully noisy as in the K–1 classroom, but it will still be full of the sounds of reading. Some students will still prefer and need to read aloud to themselves in a quiet reading voice, while others will now prefer to read more quietly.	The mood during second- and third-grade independent reading time is both joyful and intellectually stimulating. Students are reading, looking for books, talking with partners about their reading, and engaged in thinking.

Supported Independent Reading Across Grade Levels			
Grades	What It Looks Like	What It Sounds Like	What It Feels Like
4–5	Fourth- and fifth-grade classrooms will show more and more students reading individual longer books on their own. Students may house their books inside their desks or in stacks on tables. Students will also read in pairs and small groups with the teacher, but it is likely that most students in class will be independently reading in the upper-elementary grades.	Fourth and fifth grade will be more quiet during supported independent reading time. Most students will be reading quietly to themselves while the teacher is working with small groups and conferring. However, there will definitely be talk in the form of book recommendations, partner discussions, and even book club meetings. A classroom of fully engaged readers is rarely completely quiet.	The mood and feel of fourth- and fifth-grade classrooms may seem a bit serious at first, but if a visitor were to pop in and chat with students about their reading, they might learn about a funny event that just took place in a novel or a newly learned scientific theory from a nonfiction article!

INCORPORATING STATIONS INTO INDEPENDENT READING TIME

Reading-focused stations are a common teaching practice during independent reading time, especially in K–2 classrooms. Debbie Diller, author of a series of books on literacy stations, defines them as "a small defined space (portable or stationary) where students practice with a partner" (2020). In reading-focused stations, students will practice reading and engage in activities that support their reading. The reading work in stations should be familiar and highly engaging. And while students are in stations, the teacher can call small groups together for differentiated, targeted instruction.

CLASSROOM STRUCTURES TO MAKE THE MOST OF INDEPENDENT READING TIME

- **Predictability:** Supported independent reading should take place at a predictable time each day. Choose the time based on your teaching schedule, and then stick to it to the best of your ability. Regardless of what pops up— and things always pop up!—independent reading must be nonnegotiable.
- **Soft starts:** Consider more than one independent reading period a day or plan two sessions for it. One way to do this is with a soft start (Ahmed & Daniels, 2014). In soft starts, students come into the classroom, take care of all needs (putting backpacks away, ordering lunch, etc.), and then just enjoy some casual, choice, independent reading time for 15 to 30 minutes. This is in addition to instructional reading time later in the day.

- **Structured choice of seating:** Students will sustain reading for longer periods when they are in a physically comfortable position. At any given moment during reading time in my own classroom, a couple of students are at standing desks, some are lying on their stomachs and propped up with their elbows, and others are seated at tabletops. The key is not inviting students to sit anywhere they like, but rather inviting them to find a spot where they can focus for a certain period of time.
- **Stretch break:** Remaining in one position for a sustained period is difficult. Consider doing a whole-group, 30-second stretch break during longer independent reading periods.
- **Part free-choice reading, part focused reading:** While choice reading is truly what creates readers, there are times when students need to read within a certain genre, leveled text band, or topic. Consider how you might structure this for students. Many teachers have found success with asking students to read their "instructional" books for the first part of reading time and their choice books for the second part.

Great Resources

- *Simply Stations: Independent Reading* by Debbie Diller (Corwin, 2020)
- *No More Independent Reading Without Support* by Debbie Miller and Barbara Moss (Heinemann, 2013)

Notes

What Are Some Different Structures for Small-Group Learning?

Here I am, teaching a guided reading group with second graders Alexander, Amia, and Sam.

Small-group reading is often the most engaging part of a school day for students! It is the time when they get to share books, stories, and conversations with their classmates and teacher. It is also a highly effective method of instruction, as students receive targeted, in-the-moment coaching and feedback.

	Guided Reading Groups (Typically K–3)	Strategy Groups (All Grade Levels)	Book Clubs (Typically 2–5)
Purpose	To support students in continually growing their reading skills over time so they can access more complex texts	To support students in practicing and even mastering a reading strategy	To grow students' love of reading while collaborating with peers and building on their learned reading skills and strategies
Number of students in the group	2–5	2–5	2–5
When	Ongoing	Ongoing	A few times each school year
Meeting frequency	2–5 times a week, based on need	Typically 1–2 times per week or as needed	1–3 times a week
Length of time	10–15 minutes	7–12 minutes	15–30 minutes

Small-Group Tips

- Students frequently move in and out of each type of group throughout the year, flexibly and fluidly. Fixed groups do not have instructional or social-emotional benefits. In fact, they can even be damaging.
- Avoid naming groups. Because groups are fluid, it is a best practice to call students to their group meeting time by their own names rather than a fixed group name. Book club groups can be named for the title of the book or a name decided by students.

GUIDED READING GROUPS

Guided reading groups are typically determined by instructional book levels. Students reading books within the same instructional level or band of levels practice reading the same book at their own pace with teacher coaching. All students in the group read from the same text. A guided reading lesson often starts with the teacher modeling a reading strategy and then moves into students practicing that and other strategies on their own. As students read, the teacher listens in on each one to offer tips and coaching. At the end of reading the book once or twice in the group session, students and the teacher will discuss the book or the strategy they just practiced.

Guided Reading Group Tips

- Avoid the common pitfall of guided reading groups turning into small-group, round-robin, or choral reading. To do this, stagger each student's reading start time by about 5 to 10 seconds. Here's how it works:

  - One student will start reading, and the others will wait for you to give them the go-ahead to start.
  - After about 5 to 10 seconds, cue the next student to start reading. Once the next student starts reading, the first keeps reading at their own pace, and so on.
  - By staggering reading start times, students are spending the entire time reading at their own pace rather than stopping to listen to others read or reading chorally all together. This will allow you to individually coach students while the others in the group are independently reading, practicing the strategy you just taught.

- Invite students to keep their guided reading book, now a familiar book, in their book bags or boxes for them to revisit during supported independent reading time.

STRATEGY GROUPS

In strategy groups, students read their own choice independent reading books. Teachers choose students for the group based on a reading skill or strategy from which they will benefit. For example, if the class is working in a realistic fiction unit, and the teacher notices that four different students might benefit from support in identifying the problem and solution in a short story, she might create a strategy group to explicitly model how to do this. Once the teacher explains and models how to identify the problem and solution in a familiar classroom read-aloud book, students will practice doing this using their own short stories as the teacher coaches in.

Strategy Group Tips

- Book levels have no impact on strategy groups. Each student in the group might be reading a book at a different text level.
- At the end of each group meeting, invite students to share how they used the strategy in their reading.
- Plan a certain number of group meetings with an end goal. For example, a goal might sound like this: By the end of three meetings, each student will confidently name the problem and solution in their own chosen short stories.

BOOK CLUBS

While guided reading groups and strategy groups are carefully planned and led by the teacher, in book clubs, students should have more ownership and decision-making power. Students should have a choice of which book to read and even what to discuss in their book club on their meeting days. There are many formats and structures book clubs can take on. The main objective of book clubs is for students to read and talk with each other about their books. Tasks, worksheets, and projects to keep a group busy do not have a place in authentic book clubs.

Book Club Tips

- Prior to starting book clubs with students, give book talks on the books that are being offered for clubs. After the book talks, give students time (usually one entire reading period) to preview each book by reading the front/back covers and the first few pages. I invite students to rank their book choices. Then, place students in clubs based on their first- or second-ranked book, using your judgment.
- Either set a reading schedule for students or invite students to determine which page they will read to before each book club meeting so they are all discussing the same segments of text in their meetings. At the start of the school year, you may want to set the reading schedule for students, then over time invite them to work as a group to create their own reading schedule.

Great Resources

Breathing New Life Into Book Clubs: A Practical Guide for Teachers by Dr. Sonja Cherry-Paul and Dana Johansen (Heinemann, 2019)

Guided Reading, Second Edition by Irene Fountas and Gay Su Pinnell (Heinemann, 2016)

Simply Small Groups: Differentiating Literacy Learning in Any Setting by Debbie Diller (Corwin, 2021)

What Are You Grouping For? Grades 3–8: How to Guide Small Groups Based on Readers—Not the Book by Julie Wright and Barry Hoonan (Corwin, 2018)

How Does a Reading Conference Go?

WHAT IS A READING CONFERENCE?

Ms. Stephanie conferring with first-grader Mateo.

There is no teaching practice as impactful for students as the one-to-one reading conference. The conference is when you can pull up alongside a reader with wonder and awe to learn all that you can in the moment about their strengths and potential possible next steps for growth. It is the time when you will give your undivided attention to one student to engage in a learning conversation around reading.

Conferring frequently and consistently provides individual instruction to students. The conference is the teacher's perfect opportunity to provide a quick lesson to a student that the rest of the class may not need at that moment in time. Conferences are short, frequent, and centered around each individual reader. Conferences are not based on the curriculum; rather, they are based on specific learning strengths and needs.

HOW DO I CONDUCT A READING CONFERENCE?

Conferences do not necessarily need to follow a formula. However, when you are ready to start engaging in more-structured instructional conferences with students, consider practicing the steps seen in The Basic Steps of a Reading Conference chart.

The Basic Steps of a Reading Conference

1. Start with wonder.	2. Name what the reader is doing well.	3. Possibly offer a next step for growth.	4. Jot a note to yourself.
When approaching a conference with a student, listen first with awe and wonder. You might ask some of the following questions: "What are you working on as a reader?" "What would you like to talk about today?" "May I listen to you read a little bit?" Then, it's important to listen!	When listening with wonder and awe, seek out what is going well and then name it. Maybe you'll say, "You are doing something strategic in your reading; you are _____."	Some conferences will end with naming a reading strength and then jotting a note. In others, you will offer a next step for growth. It might sound like this: "You're ready for a next step as a reader. When you are reading, you can try to _____." You might model what you are asking your students to try. Then, invite them to try it and offer support or coaching if necessary.	After your conference, jot a quick note to remind yourself for future reference and planning what you talked about with your students.

Chart modified from *To Know and Nurture a Reader: Conferring With Confidence and Joy* by Kari Yates and Christina Nosek (Stenhouse, 2018).

Tip

Consider leaving a reminder of learning on a sticky note for students to keep in their reading notebook or folder.

A sticky-note reminder from a second-grade conference

Because conferences are individualized for the strengths and needs of each student, they will take more time in the classroom than other teaching methods like small- and whole-group lessons. A good place to start figuring out how to fit conferences into your teaching schedule to is create a weekly plan (Appendix G). To get started, plan to meet with individual students once per week. Then, as you become more knowledgeable in your students' strengths and needs, you can adjust the timing of when you meet with them. Some students will benefit from more conferences while others may not need as many.

Great Resource

To Know and Nurture a Reader: Conferring With Confidence and Joy by Kari Yates and Christina Nosek (Stenhouse, 2018)

Tip

If conferring with readers is new to you, it is most important to skip the steps to start and just engage in casual conversation with each of your readers. Once you're comfortable with that, give the basic steps a try!

Notes

How Can I Incorporate Reading Throughout the Entire School Day?

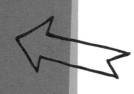

Ms. Cohen was searching for a way to make her science lessons more engaging and impactful. She found herself using her school's adopted textbook and workbook, but she felt that her students were not exactly engaged in the lessons. When talking about this concern with her school's literacy coach, he suggested using topical picture books to liven up subject area instruction. So Ms. Cohen consulted the librarian at her community library to seek out picture books about magnetism, her current science unit. She was thrilled when the librarian led her to discover 12 picture books in the children's section! She knew that there was so much she could do to liven up her science instruction with these new-to-her picture books.

In elementary classrooms, reading plays a role in absolutely everything. Students who read proficiently and confidently find more success in the other subjects in school. From reading directions and story problems in math to navigating a science textbook, learning in all other subject areas is often dependent on students' ability to read. Including reading instruction throughout the school day will support students across all of their learning, and all it takes are a few simple shifts!

SIMPLE WAYS TO INCORPORATE READING INSTRUCTION INTO ALL SUBJECT AREAS

- **Plan picture book interactive read alouds throughout the school day in different subject areas.** Try planning an interactive read aloud around an idea in one of your content areas. Countless picture books have been written around topics in all content areas for all grade levels. As Ms. Cohen did, you can ask your school or local librarian for recommendations. Additionally, Appendix E lists online sources for finding children's literature, including content area picture books.
- **Create topic-specific text sets.** Gather lots of picture books from the school or public library around a current or upcoming unit of study. When creating a text set around a topic, choose books across a range of reading levels and modalities (graphic texts, picture books, chapter books, novels, poetry books, etc.) so that all students are able to find topic-specific books that they can read and want to read. Introduce students to each of the books by doing short book talks. Then, include the books in an accessible book basket or two in your classroom library. Of those 12 books on magnetism that Ms. Cohen found at the library, she used two as interactive read alouds and the other 10 in a text set book basket on magnetism.

How Can I Incorporate Reading Throughout the Entire School Day?

93

Ms. Cohen's magnetism text set book box

● **Strategically use co-created teaching charts.** An important reading skill for students is to learn how and where to access needed information. Teaching charts are the entry point into this important work. The teaching chart is one of my favorite instructional tools that spans subjects, topics, and all grade levels. Kate Roberts and Maggie Beattie-Roberts (2016) remind us that charts are not the teaching itself; rather, charts are a reminder of the teaching so the learning can be referenced (or re-read) again and again. The most effective charts are the ones students and teachers co-create. Teaching charts co-created with students can show strategies taught, step-by-step directions, explanations of concepts, lists of important terminology, and much more. Plus, if students and teachers co-create a written chart with visuals, students will feel ownership and thus will be more likely to read the chart and refer to it again and again. Ms. Cohen and her students created this chart about magnetism after reading one of the books she found at the library and experimenting with magnets and different objects.

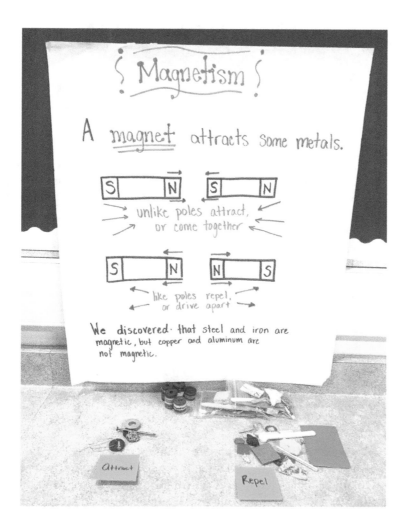

- **Introduce students to potentially unfamiliar vocabulary with each new topic in the subject areas.** Talk about what the words mean, keep an accessible list of the words accompanying pictures displayed in the classroom, and show multiple images or actual objects themselves if possible. Invite students to be on the lookout for these words while learning. Additionally, encourage students to use the words in discussion. Model this by frequently using the words yourself. Ms. Cohen and her class created a list of magnetism words that was displayed in the classroom and often referenced during science lessons.

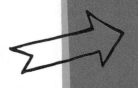

What Are Some Special Considerations in the K–1 Classroom?

Kindergarten and first-grade students come to school with already rich, literate lives. Whether through shared family stories, verbal exchanges between siblings and cousins, or listening and singing along to favorite songs, all of your students' lived literacy experiences will enhance your classroom! For some students, this might be their first experience with a teacher guiding and coaching them. Therefore, it is critical that you spend time getting to know your young learners and honoring who they are and where they come from in the pursuit of learning.

Although kindergarten and first-grade classrooms are not where reading identities are always first formed, they are often the places where these identities are either validated and nurtured or devalued and hindered. So first and foremost, reading must be a joyful and engaging experience for kindergarten and first-grade learners.

The primary grades are critical in developing the early skills of reading: how to decode print and how to learn what reading sounds like, and why we do it (to make meaning). These are the foundations on which all other reading experiences will build in school.

In addition to the key instructional principles mentioned throughout this chapter, other forms of reading instruction will also take place in kindergarten and first-grade classrooms. On any given day, students may engage in some or all of these reading practices: a shared read in the form of a poem; imaginative free-choice playtime, full of opportunities for listening and speaking to others; a short lesson where the teacher models a strategy; guided reading groups and conferences; phonological awareness practice with a rhyming game; an engaging interactive read aloud; a playful yet intentional phonics lesson; and an additional read aloud just to enjoy a story together as a community of readers.

> *Remember: Comprehension is the ultimate goal of reading instruction!* All of the considerations and components in the K–1 reading classroom are taught and practiced in the service of making meaning. Kindergarteners and first graders need to understand that readers turn pages in books, listen for sounds, and name words in phrases to create meaning—maybe to follow a story or learn something new and interesting.

CONSIDERATIONS AND COMPONENTS IN THE K–1 READING CLASSROOM

The following text contains a rundown of key considerations and components for K–1 teachers to consider, along with Great Resources where you can find more thorough information and helpful strategies.

PLAY

Time for imaginative play is often left out of classrooms. Yet anyone who has spent any time with 5-, 6-, and 7-year-olds knows the power and benefits of play. Not only does it break up the academic day by providing movement and choice for our youngest learners, but it also supports them in developing speaking, listening, and even comprehension skills (Mraz et al., 2016).

ORAL LANGUAGE DEVELOPMENT

Kindergarten and first-grade classrooms should be overflowing with opportunities for both structured and unstructured oral language development. Essentially, students should have ongoing experiences throughout each day for speaking and listening, which ultimately benefit their reading and writing development. After all, comprehension of printed text is dependent on the comprehension of oral language. Students will likely not understand a word in print if they have never heard or spoken it before.

CONCEPTS OF PRINT

Concepts of print are essentially "the rules of the road" for reading (Clay, 2000). Concepts of print include, but are not limited to, holding a book in the correct orientation, locating the front and back cover, turning a single page at a time from right to left, locating the starting point for reading on a page, and reading text and pictures from left to right/top to bottom. Many kindergarten and some first-grade students will need a little extra boost with these skills.

PHONOLOGICAL AWARENESS, PHONEMIC AWARENESS, AND PHONICS

Much has been written and debated about the role of phonological awareness, phonemic awareness, and phonics instruction. These terms are often misunderstood and misused, so embarking on a deep dive into understanding them is essential for all K–1 teachers. The scope of this book will not cover these elements to the degree that is needed for teachers of early literacy, so I highly recommend taking the time to read and learn more about these critical early-reading building blocks.

- **Phonological awareness** is the ability to recognize and manipulate sounds in spoken language. It is often thought of as the umbrella term for all things having to do with the sound/language relationship.
- **Phonemic awareness** is the most specific form of phonological awareness. It refers to sounds at the word level, specifically sound/letter correspondence.
- **Phonics** refers to the correspondence of the sounds in spoken language and the printed letters and words that comprise text.

Keep in Mind

Instruction in phonemic awareness and phonics should be fun and engaging! Songs, chants, poems, games, and kinesthetic activities can all play a role in the learning of these critical foundational skills.

BOOK BOXES OR BAGS

Young readers will need lots of books! Provide each reader with their own book bag or box full of books they can read and want to read both at school and home. Their book bags/boxes should include familiar, decodable, and high-interest books. Switch out the books every week or so. Additionally, kindergarten and first-grade readers may also need alphabet charts, sight words, reading mats, and other reading tools.

This first grader's book box holds books that she chose with her teacher's support from a browsing box, in addition to a few decodable books, high-interest books from the classroom library, a ring of sight words, and a sticky-note reminder from a guided reading lesson.

FAMILIAR BOOKS

Familiar books are books first read by the teacher and then given to students for continued re-reading. The reading and frequent re-reading of familiar books in kindergarten and first-grade classrooms is a critical component of supporting young readers' growth. Elizabeth Sulzby's (1985) work on emergent storybook reading tells us that quite a bit can be learned when students read loved, familiar books again and again, including learning how stories sound, how pictures tell a story, and that reading is a joyful experience!

Kathy Collins and Matt Glover (2015) took this idea one step further, stating that familiar books do not necessarily need to be driven by the teacher only. Students have their own loved books and stories that need to be honored. Reading a loved book multiple times, even hundreds of times, not only grows a child's love of reading, but it also is a consistent launching point for students to practice the strategies and skills of reading that they are being taught in class. After all, kids are more likely to independently practice reading strategies in books they are motivated to read.

DECODABLE BOOKS

In addition to familiar books, students in kindergarten and first grade should have access to high-quality decodable books. Decodable books are books in which students can successfully decode and recognize all words. They are comprised of words made up of letter/sound or grapheme/sound correspondences that students have already learned and can successfully practice over and over again. Not only do these books build fluency because of students' reading accuracy, but they also build confidence in young readers and support letter–sound relationships and orthographic mapping. High-quality decodable books can be challenging to find. Many teachers and specialists have started creating their own.

Terms to Know

Grapheme: How sound, or a phoneme, is represented in print. For example, the grapheme "s" represents the first sound heard in the word "sit" and the last sound heard in the word "cats." Graphemes can be made up of one, two, three, or even four letters, as in the grapheme "eigh" in the word "eight"; "eigh" is only one of a few graphemes that make the sound /ā/.

HIGH-INTEREST BOOKS

It is unlikely that most kindergarten or first-grade students will be able to read every word in a detailed book about dinosaurs or in a book featuring the latest stars of soccer. However, if students are interested in dinosaurs or soccer, they should have access to those books. Not only will students find engagement in the images in the texts, but they will also work to solve many words and will start to realize what they have to look forward to in their reading future! Plus, reading high-interest books will support students' oral language development. After all, there is a lot to discuss in high-interest books!

BROWSING BOXES

To make sure students are reading books they want to read at their current independent and instructional text level, consider using browsing boxes. In her first-grade classroom, Haley curates browsing boxes at her students' independent and instructional levels and keeps them behind her small-group table for easy access during and after lessons.

This is the reading area in Haley's first-grade classroom. Everything she needs for teaching reading is at her fingertips.

Scan the QR code to learn how first-grade teacher Haley uses browsing boxes with her students.

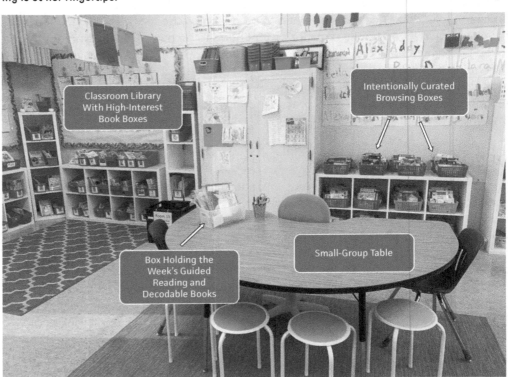

Classroom Library With High-Interest Book Boxes

Intentionally Curated Browsing Boxes

Box Holding the Week's Guided Reading and Decodable Books

Small-Group Table

Great Resources

How to Support Students Who Are Not Yet Conventionally Reading

- *I Am Reading* by Kathy Collins and Matt Glover (Heinemann, 2015)

Incorporating Play

- *Purposeful Play* by Kristine Mraz, Alison Porceli, and Cheryl Tyler (Heinemann, 2016)

Concepts of Print

- *Concepts About Print, Second Edition* by Marie Clay (Heinemann, 2017)

Phonological Awareness, Phonemic Awareness, and Phonics

- *Shifting the Balance* by Jan Burkins and Kari Yates (Stenhouse, 2021)

- *How to Prevent Reading Difficulties* by Mark Weakland (Corwin, 2021)

- *A Fresh Look at Phonics* by Wiley Blevins (Corwin, 2017)

chapter
FOUR

HOW DO I USE ASSESSMENT IN THE SERVICE OF STUDENTS?

Ms. Flaherty, a teacher of two years, is wondering if she has enough information about her students to help them better progress as readers. She is doing everything required by her school—giving a monthly computerized reading assessment and benchmark assessment every two to three months—yet she feels she does not have enough specific information about her students to inform her reading instruction on a daily basis. She wants to better know her readers so she can more effectively give them what they need to continue to grow. She knows that strategic formative assessment will lead her to develop more intentional instruction for her readers. However, she isn't quite sure where to start.

Like Ms. Flaherty, many teachers aren't sure where to start when it comes to getting to fully know their readers' strengths and areas of need for more support. This chapter aims to make it clearer.

As an elementary teacher, you will not assess your readers to assign grades; rather, you assess them to guide you on where to go with your instruction to best support their needs and strengths. Formative assessment and instruction are inherently linked. The pages ahead emphasize the importance of getting to know each of your readers' individual strengths and areas of needed support using a multitude of methods of formative assessment of reading.

Eight of Your Biggest Questions About Using Assessment in the Service of Students

1. What is formative assessment in reading instruction?

2. How do I approach assessment from an asset-based perspective?

3. What are some common formative assessment methods?

4. How do I keep track of my students' different strengths and next steps as readers?

5. How will I know what to assess?

6. How will I know when to expect mastery?

7. How can I assess if students are understanding while I'm teaching?

8. What do I do if I feel a student may need extra support outside of classroom time?

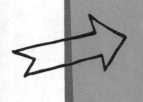

What Is Formative Assessment in Reading Instruction?

The consistent use of formative assessment is your greatest tool as a reading teacher. Formative assessment directly informs your teaching choices and decisions. It is based on the needs and strengths that you observe in your students' reading. Regular use of formative assessment is your path to being a reflective, responsive reading teacher.

Formative Assessment Is . . .	Formative Assessment Is *Not* . . .
A tool to inform planning for in-the-moment and future teaching.	A means for assigning a score or grade.
Flexible and versatile. There are many different forms and methods.	A fixed method.
Sometimes planned and other times spontaneous and in the moment.	Always a formal or planned process.
Ongoing. It never stops.	Something done once a day, week, or even periodically.

Terms to Know

Formative assessment: Has the goal of informing instruction based on observation and evidence to enhance student learning.

Summative assessment: Has the goal of evaluating student learning, typically to assign a score or grade.

When you approach teaching with the constant lens of formative assessment, you are always asking yourself these questions:

1   What are my students doing and understanding?
2   How should I respond?
3   Is my response supporting my students' ability to do and understand?

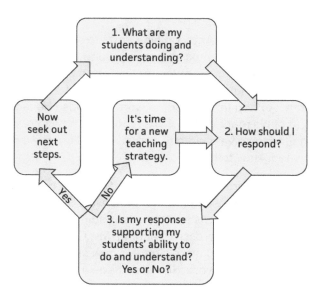

The following two examples from the classroom describe the power and impact of using formative assessment.

EXAMPLE OF ASSESSMENT INFORMING FUTURE TEACHING

1 *What are my students doing and understanding?*
   When discussing character traits during an interactive read aloud, Mr. Sinosa noticed that many of the responses from his students were not based on the character's actions or words, but rather how the character appears in the pictures. This noticing informed his teaching for the next lesson.

2 *How should I respond?*
   Mr. Sinosa debated between creating a couple of small strategy groups to directly teach identifying traits based on a character's actions and words or doing another interactive read aloud, this time directly pointing out to students how a character's words and actions can help readers identify some of their character traits. He opted for the interactive read aloud.

3 *Is my response supporting my students' ability to do and understand?*
   After the interactive read aloud the next day, Mr. Sinosa noticed that most of the class was now responding in the way he had hoped. He also identified four students who would further benefit from a strategy group on identifying character traits and planned that strategy group for the next day.

EXAMPLE OF ASSESSMENT INFORMING IN-THE-MOMENT TEACHING

1 *What are my students doing and understanding?*
   During a reading conference with Andy, Ms. Carter noticed he was fluently reading with an expressive voice, but that he was not consistently reading through entire multisyllabic words or monitoring for meaning while he read those words. For example, instead of reading the word "elements," he read "elementary." Instead of reading "something," he read "sometimes." This observation during the conference led Ms. Carter to her next steps.

ASSESSMENT

2   *How should I respond?*
    Ms. Carter complimented Andy on his efforts to read with a fluent, expressive voice. Then, she offered a next step, suggesting that Andy make the effort to consistently monitor for meaning, notice when something doesn't make sense, and work to make it make sense. Andy stated that he wasn't stopping to spend time working through some words because he didn't want to mess up the sound of his reading. Ms. Carter modeled how to re-read a sentence after taking time to solve a word to continue the fluent, expressive reading. She then invited Andy to try.

3   *Is my response supporting my students' ability to do and understand?*
    After Ms. Carter's response in the moment, Andy tried it. He spent time reading through entire words and then re-reading the sentence to both preserve meaning and expressive reading. Ms. Carter ended the conference by reminding Andy to keep practicing this new skill he just learned each time he stops to solve a tricky word. She also made a note to check back in with Andy during their small-group work the next day.

In both of these classroom examples, the teachers used formative assessment to directly inform their teaching. The first example with Mr. Sinosa showed how formative assessment can support decisions about future teaching. The second example with Ms. Carter demonstrated how formative assessment can be used to inform teaching in the moment.

Notes

WHAT IS AN ASSET-BASED PERSPECTIVE?

An asset-based perspective refers to looking for and noticing what students are already doing well. It's seeking out the many positives that already exist and persist in each of our students. In her 2020 book *Cultivating Genius: An Equity Framework for Culturally and Historically Responsive Literacy*, Gholdy Muhammad offers that "history from Black communities tells us that educators don't need to empower youth or give them brilliance or genius. Instead, the power and genius is already within them" (p. 13). Just imagine the great shift in our schools if all school personnel approached students with this powerful belief and perspective.

The children in your classroom come to you with so much to share, offer, and achieve. Rather than focusing on what a student is *not* doing, reframe your thinking to ask what a student *is* doing and how you can use that to support them in continuing to thrive and grow. All of your students enter your classroom with many assets. Your most important job as a teacher is to recognize those assets and support students in building upon them.

Five Key Principles to Shifting to an Asset-Based Perspective

1. Internalize the truth that all students already have highly developed interests, reading habits, skills, and strategies.

2. Make an effort to seek out and notice those interests, reading habits, skills, and strategies.

3. Intentionally name and acknowledge all of your students' noticed assets so they will continue to use them and recognize that their teacher sees and believes in them.

4. Rather than viewing things students are *not* doing as readers, reframe this thinking as possible next steps to teach to help students grow.

5. Always seek your students' input. Offer frequent opportunities for them to share their assets and what they feel their possible next steps may be.

To shift your words and actions to an asset-based perspective, it is first important to start shifting your thoughts and mindset. Start looking for what students *are* doing successfully. Pay attention to their approximations and small steps toward progress. Instead of telling students what they are *not* doing, invite them to practice next steps to help them continually grow as readers. A few simple language and thought swaps will help with this reframing shift.

ASSESSMENT

Observation	Instead of Thinking/ Saying . . .	Reframe Your Thoughts and Words
As Mei is reading aloud, she uses beautiful inflection within phrases but is not yet pausing at periods.	Mei is not pausing at periods when she reads.	Mei uses such beautiful expression as she reads. She's now ready for a next step as a reader. To make her reading sound more like talking, I can teach her to pause each time she comes to a period.
Wilson often chats off-topic during partner reading time.	Wilson needs to stay on task and stop talking.	Wilson is a reader who values conversations with a partner. To make the most of those conversations, I can support him in generating a list of things he and his partner can talk about during reading time to continue to help him grow as a reader.
Deshaun seems to consistently gravitate toward graphic novels and other highly visual texts.	Deshaun reads too many graphic novels. He needs to read more variety.	Deshaun is a reader who finds value in visual texts. I should honor what he values while also introducing him to new texts, such as graphic nonfiction and illustration-rich fiction that I think might line up with his interests.

Notes

Answers to Your Biggest Questions About Teaching Elementary Reading

What Are Some Common Formative Assessment Methods?

Formative assessment is extremely versatile. There are many different methods that can be used concurrently in the classroom to inform your instructional decisions. The Common Formative Assessment Methods table offers seven common forms of formative assessment in the reading classroom.

Common Formative Assessment Methods		
Formative Assessment Method	**When Is It Done?**	**Why Is It Powerful?**
Observation from a distance	When students are independently reading or working in reading stations	Observation from a distance enables you to notice reading behaviors and quickly identify who may need immediate and quick support.
Discussion during lessons and read alouds	During whole-group and small-group instructional times, including read aloud	Discussion offers you the opportunity to clue into students' thinking and response to others' thinking around reading.
Observation up close and listening to reading	Anytime students are reading in any format: conferences during independent reading, small groups, in stations, in partnerships	Up-close observation and listening to reading allows you to home in on reading behaviors and skill and strategy use at close range. You'll be able to respond in the moment or jot notes to keep track of patterns over time.
Conferring	Every supported independent reading period	Talking with individual students about their reading offers insight into their thinking about reading. It also enables you to pinpoint their specific strengths and needs in the moment and talk about learning goals.
Running records* (Clay, 2017)	During conferences or small groups	Running records enable you to track and respond to students' reading accuracy, errors, and self-corrections in the moment and over time as you notice patterns.

ASSESSMENT

Common Formative Assessment Methods		
Formative Assessment Method	**When Is It Done?**	**Why Is It Powerful?**
Reading student writing about reading	During or any time after students write, jot, or sketch about their reading	Student writing, jotting, and sketching about reading can offer an insight into their understanding and thinking. However, talking with students about their reading is often a more accurate assessment of comprehension.

*The running record is a powerful tool that enables teachers to see exactly what students are doing as readers while they are reading. Learning how to take and analyze running records goes well beyond the scope of this book. It is a powerful reading practice all elementary educators should adopt.
To learn more about running records, I recommend Marie Clay's(*Running Records for Classroom Teachers* (2017).

Notes

How Do I Keep Track of My Students' Different Strengths and Next Steps as Readers?

Assessing is one thing. Keeping track of all your formative assessment observations, notes, and insights is another. The power of formative assessment will only be fully realized if you either use it to teach in the moment or have a record to refer to that will inform future teaching.

There are many methods for keeping track of your formative assessment notes. The best method for formative assessment note-taking is the method that you will stick with consistently over time. Some teachers prefer a digital route while others use paper and pen. Over the years, I have tried many different methods for note-taking, and only one has stuck for me: paper notes in a binder or on a clipboard.

Keeping my trusty clipboard by my side during reading time has helped me take notes at a moment's notice. Whether I am working with students in small groups, engaging in a reading conference, or even listening in during a partner talk portion of a lesson, my clipboard is at-the-ready to house all of my ongoing formative assessment observations, notes, and insights.

I find three different forms to be useful and needed when keeping formative assessment notes. All of these are available in the appendices:

1   A class list with checkboxes
2   Three Goals Formative Assessment Form
3   Individual student assessment forms

CLASS LIST WITH CHECKBOXES

The class list with checkboxes (Appendix H) enables you to keep track of how often you have met with students. It's a great tool for jotting the date of each time you confer or meet in a small group with a student. What I find most useful about this tool is that you can easily see who you have and haven't met with each week. In the image on page 112, you can see which students I have met with most frequently and who I still need to meet with. Not all students will need to meet with you at the same frequency, but all students do need to meet with you in conferences or small groups each week.

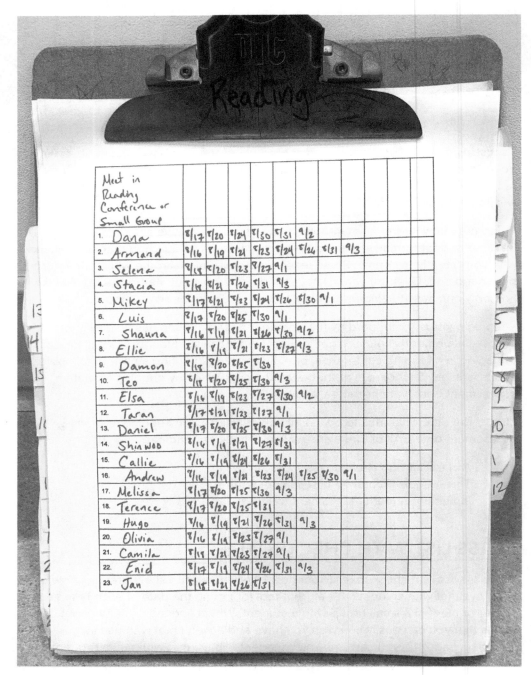

Meet in Reading Conference or Small Group								
1. Dana	8/17	8/20	8/24	8/30	8/31	9/2		
2. Armand	8/16	8/19	8/21	8/23	8/24	8/26	8/31	9/3
3. Selena	8/18	8/20	8/23	8/27	9/1			
4. Stacia	8/18	8/21	8/26	8/31	9/3			
5. Mikey	8/17	8/21	8/23	8/24	8/26	8/30	9/1	
6. Luis	8/17	8/20	8/25	8/30	9/1			
7. Shauna	8/16	8/19	8/21	8/26	8/30	9/2		
8. Ellie	8/16	8/19	8/21	8/23	8/27	9/3		
9. Damon	8/18	8/20	8/25	8/30				
10. Teo	8/18	8/20	8/25	8/30	9/3			
11. Elsa	8/16	8/19	8/23	8/27	8/30	9/2		
12. Taran	8/17	8/21	8/23	8/27	9/1			
13. Daniel	8/17	8/20	8/25	8/30	9/3			
14. Shin Woo	8/16	8/19	8/21	8/27	8/31			
15. Callie	8/16	8/19	8/24	8/26	8/31			
16. Andrew	8/16	8/19	8/21	8/23	8/24	8/25	8/30	9/1
17. Melissa	8/17	8/20	8/25	8/30	9/3			
18. Terence	8/17	8/20	8/25	8/31				
19. Hugo	8/16	8/19	8/21	8/26	8/31	9/3		
20. Olivia	8/16	8/19	8/23	8/27	9/1			
21. Camila	8/18	8/21	8/23	8/27	9/1			
22. Enid	8/17	8/19	8/24	8/26	8/31	9/3		
23. Jan	8/18	8/21	8/26	8/31				

Class checkbox grid over three weeks of conferring and small groups

THREE GOALS FORMATIVE ASSESSMENT FORM

Before you start each reading unit, consider selecting three learning targets that your entire class will master by the end of the unit. While every student will work toward more than three goals and most will master more than three goals, the goals chosen before the start of the unit will be the ones your reading community collectively works toward as a group. At the start of the unit, formatively assess students and write their names in pencil in the appropriate boxes on the Three Goals Formative Assessment Form (see Appendix I). Depending on the goals you choose, this can usually be done with a quick check-in conference with each

Answers to Your Biggest Questions About Teaching Elementary Reading

student. As children grow and progress throughout the unit, erase their names and write them in the top box. The goal at the end of the unit is to have all children's names in the top boxes.

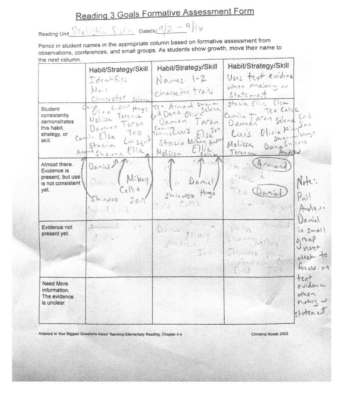

Three Goals Formative Assessment Form at the beginning and end of a unit. Notice how growth is recorded over time by moving the student names in the columns. Also notice that the teacher jotted next steps in the side margin after seeing that two students still need support in one area.

INDIVIDUAL STUDENT ASSESSMENT FORM

The assessment form I use to keep specific details about individual students' strengths and needs is the Individual Student Assessment Form (Appendix J). I keep one form per student on my clipboard. To easily find a student's page on the clipboard, I place a small sticky note with the student's name or number on the side of the page.

This form is adapted from a form Kari Yates and I created in *To Know and Nurture a Reader* (2018). The form is a four-square grid where you can keep assessment notes about four specific areas of reading. You will decide which four areas to formatively assess over a period of time, depending on your current reading unit or every month or so. Some general examples of what four things may be assessed are as follows:

- Book choice, reading habits, strategic process, authentic response (Yates & Nosek, 2018)
- Decoding, fluency, basic comprehension, extended thinking

There are times in the classroom when you'll need to be more specific with your formative assessment, so the terms you write in the grid will be less general, such as in these examples:

- Primary grades: reading material organization, reading stamina, talk about text, talk about own ideas
- Upper grades: stating a detailed opinion, using evidence to support the opinion, acknowledging a counter opinion, stating a reasoned rebuttal

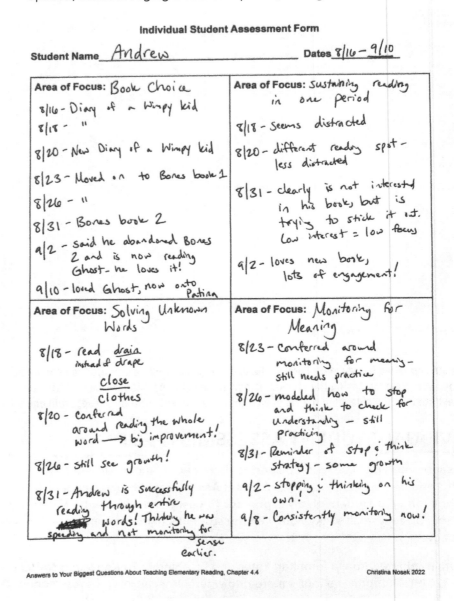

Individual Student Assessment Form

Student Name _Andrew_   Dates _8/16 – 9/10_

Area of Focus: Book Choice	Area of Focus: Sustaining reading in one period
8/16 - Diary of a Wimpy kid	8/18 - Seems distracted
8/18 - "	8/20 - different reading spot - less distracted
8/20 - New Diary of a Wimpy kid	8/31 - clearly is not interested in his books, but is trying to stick it out. Low interest = low focus
8/23 - Moved on to Bones book 1	
8/26 - "	
8/31 - Bones book 2	
9/2 - said he abandoned Bones 2 and is now reading Ghost - he loves it!	9/2 - loves new book, lots of engagement!
9/10 - loved Ghost, now onto Patina	
Area of Focus: Solving Unknown Words	**Area of Focus: Monitoring for Meaning**
8/18 - read drain instead of drape	8/23 - Conferred around monitoring for meaning - still needs practice
close / clothes	8/26 - modeled how to stop and think to check for understanding - still practicing
8/20 - Conferred around reading the whole word → big improvement!	8/31 - Reminder of stop & think strategy - some growth
8/26 - still see growth!	9/2 - stopping & thinking on his own!
8/31 - Andrew is successfully reading through entire words! Thinking he was speeding and not monitoring for sense earlier.	9/8 - Consistently monitoring now!

Answers to Your Biggest Questions About Teaching Elementary Reading, Chapter 4.4   Christina Nosek 2022

Notes about formative assessment observations and teaching with one student

Consistent use of these three forms over time will support your work in spotting patterns in your students' strengths and next steps. Based on what you notice, you will be able to create more effective small groups and tailor your instruction to meet your students' unique strengths and needs. For example, if you notice after two weeks of consistent formative assessment note-taking that four students still need support with a specific skill that the rest of the class has mastered, you can form a small group of those four to support their specific needs.

How Will I Know What to Assess?

Reading happens when many factors work together concurrently. It can be thought of like baking a cake. To bake a cake, all ingredients must be gathered, measured, combined, and baked to create an edible, delicious dessert. If the sugar is missing or measured incorrectly, the cake will not properly come together. In reading, if one of the many elements is missing or not applied consistently, reading will not come together. To determine if all the elements of reading are in place for a student, you will assess different factors of reading. Sometimes, some elements will hold more weight in your assessments than others, depending on your students' individual strengths and needs. It's typical for students to show greater strength in some areas than others as they're learning to put all the reading ingredients together.

The best way to determine what students need is to watch and listen to them read and talk about their reading. You will do this through consistent use of different assessment methods (discussed earlier in this chapter) to learn your students' individual strengths and possible next steps for your teaching.

The following chart lists the elements of reading in which you will assess and then teach as needed. *Note:* This chart offers the basic description of why each listed element of reading is important to assess.

Elements of Reading to Formatively Assess and Then Teach		
	Reading Element	**Why It's Important**
Setting up for reading success	Book choice	Students will not read at a high volume unless they know how to choose books they *can* read and *want* to read.
	Habits	Settling into a good reading spot, being able to sustain reading, and noticing when focus is lost are all habits of good readers. Sometimes, a lack of these habits can get in the way of reading.
	Self-regulation	Self-regulation in reading includes motivation, engagement, and executive-function skills. If a student is not engaged, motivated, or able to self-regulate in order to complete a focused task, reading will likely be difficult (Duke & Cartwright, 2021).

(Continued)

ASSESSMENT

(Continued)

Elements of Reading to Formatively Assess and Then Teach		
	Reading Element	**Why It's Important**
Foundational reading	Listening comprehension	If students have never or infrequently heard or used a word in speech, they likely will not be able to recognize or understand it in printed text. Background knowledge and vocabulary acquisition play a key role in listening comprehension.
	Concepts of print	In order to read, students need to know how to hold a book, turn pages, and start from the top left part of the page (Clay, 2000).
	Decoding and word recognition	Phonological awareness and phonics play principal roles in decoding and word recognition. Most students will need intentional instruction in these areas. Some students will need more intensive instruction in these areas in order to read words (Brady, 2020; Suggate, 2016).
	Fluency	Lack of automaticity, intonation, and a rate that sounds like verbal speech often play a role in hindering comprehension (Stevens et al., 2017).
	Comprehension	The purpose of reading is to make meaning, so if students are not comprehending what they are reading, further exploration to pinpoint why needs to take place through assessment.

Elements of Reading to Formatively Assess and Then Teach		
	Reading Element	**Why It's Important**
Complex thinking skills	Response and reflection	While making meaning through comprehension about what a text says is critically important, it is equally important to take it a step further with students to support them in further thinking and reflecting about a text. Seeking out if a student can recall what's in the text is only the first step in understanding. The next step involves understanding if a student is doing in-the-head and in-the-heart thinking work (Beers & Probst, 2017). This involves learning about oneself and ideas connected to life outside of the pages.

Table informed by Duke and Cartwright's *Active View of Reading* (2021) and Scarborough's (2001) rope model of reading.

The more you work with your students and get to know them as readers, the better equipped you will be to figure out where your assessment and teaching based on assessment will need to be focused. In each grade level, each of your students will show strengths and needs with the different elements of reading. You might find that some students need more support with decoding, while others need your instruction to be focused on comprehension or reflection.

In the primary grades, much but not all of your assessment will focus on foundational reading skills. In the upper grades, a shift will take place. Your assessment will not completely move away from foundational reading, but as students grow as readers, your assessment will move toward a broader focus on the deeper thinking that comes with reading more-complex texts.

Striking the perfect balance of what to assess and instruct can be tricky! One way to think about striking the right balance for the class is imagining students' individual strong reading foundations and also the skills in which they need support as a playground seesaw. Finding the right balance of assessment and instruction to level your students' metaphorical seesaws will take some work.

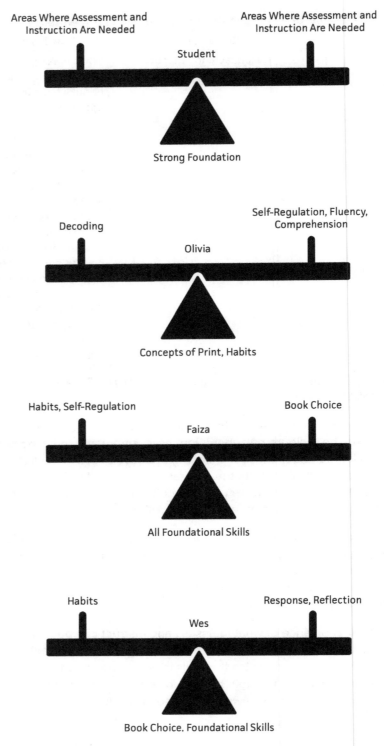

Image source: iStock.com/Rifai ozil

Imagine three students in any given elementary classroom. It's likely that each of those three students will have different reading foundations (skills they have acquired) and different needs. Ongoing formative assessment is the only way to strike the right balance of where you will focus your whole-group, small-group, and individual instruction (see Chapter 3).

In the Balance Seesaw figure, Olivia has a strong foundation in concepts of print and reading habits but needs intensive support in decoding and some support in self-regulation, fluency, and comprehension. Faiza and Wes's strong foundations and needs for support are quite different than Olivia's. Both Faiza and Wes have a strong foundation in reading foundational skills but need teaching in other areas. Through use of consistent formative assessment, their teacher is able to pinpoint and balance the instruction needed to meet the varying strengths and needs of these three different readers.

Your consistent use of formative assessment, note-taking to keep track of what you've learned about each student, and making decisions based on what you've learned will support you in the ongoing work of balancing each of your students' metaphorical reading seesaws.

Notes

ASSESSMENT

How Will I Know When to Expect Mastery?

After two days of lessons about how to view and read text features such as diagrams and maps to inform understanding of an informational text, Ms. Nguyen noticed that her students were applying the strategies taught in the lessons with different degrees of understanding. A few students seemed to have mastered the strategies, while others demonstrated a comfortable understanding. Two students still seemed unfamiliar with the concept despite the two lessons. Ms. Nguyen realized that the students who still appeared perplexed with the idea needed to be taught in a different way. So she made a note to pull the students for two small group meetings during the week to try some different strategies.

It is important to remember that mastery should not be expected immediately after each lesson for every student in your class. The path to understanding any concept can be thought of as a continuum. So even before the lesson starts, you will want to consider possible plans of action for students who may need different support or more time with a concept.

Expect and Accept Varying Paces to Mastery

Students will spend different amounts of time in each of the understanding stages.

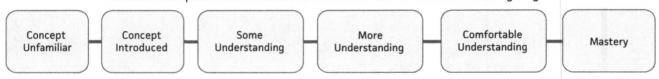

Expect and accept approximations.
Notice and adjust teaching when misunderstandings arise.

Students who are demonstrating approximations and some understanding of a concept might need more time to practice, different instruction in a small group, or more individualized instruction in a conference. When students are within this range of learning in a concept, they are within their own zone of proximal development (Vygotsky, 1978). They are ready to practice, refine, and learn the concept, which will eventually lead to mastery with both independent and supported practice over time.

When students are showing misunderstanding or unfamiliarity after you have taught a lesson, it may be time to either teach the concept in a different way or consider taking a few steps back and reevaluating what they are ready to learn. Making use of learning progressions will help you in this work. Many curriculums include learning progressions. If yours does not, you can make your own to inform your teaching using the following steps:

Step 1: Identify the skill to be mastered.

Step 2: Identify the skills needed prior to learning the mastery skill.

Step 3: Order the skills needed from first-learned skill up to the mastery skill.

How to Create a Learning Progression

Step 1: Identify the skill to be mastered.

↓

Example: Identify the main character's traits in a fictional story.

Step 2: Identify the skills needed prior to learning the mastery skill.

↓

Example:
-Define what a trait is.
-Identify the main character.
-Name common character traits.
-Name some things the character does and says in the story.

Step 3: Order the skills needed from first-learned skill up to the mastery skill.

↓

Example:
In the progression of learning leading to identifying the main character's traits, students first need to do the following:
1. Define "trait."
2. Name some common traits.
3. Identify the main character in the story.
4. Name some things the main character does and says.
5. Name a trait of the character based on what they do or say.

Notes

ASSESSMENT

How Can I Assess if Students Are Understanding While I'm Teaching?

While teaching a whole-group reading lesson about identifying the main idea in a short nonfiction text, Ms. Vasquez noticed that most of her class appeared engaged, but a few students seemed confused or disengaged. She wondered if her students understood the content she was delivering in the way she was teaching it. She knew she needed to find out and make adjustments if necessary.

If students are not engaged and learning from a lesson, the time spent teaching will not be effective. To make your teaching time as effective as possible, you will want to assess if your students are engaged and understanding in the moment during the lesson and make adjustments if necessary. While this can be a tricky task to get the hang of at first, once you become accustomed to gauging engagement and understanding it will be something that you do more and more naturally over time. There are a few quick methods you can use to assess student understanding while you are teaching a lesson.

QUICK METHODS TO ASSESS DURING A LESSON

CHECK-IN WITH THUMBS

A visual check-in with thumbs can be used to assess whether or not students are understanding at any point during the lesson. To do this, ask students to close a hand into a fist and place it on their chests. Then, ask your class something along the lines of this: *"Give a thumbs up, thumbs down, or thumb somewhere in the middle to show your understanding. Give a thumbs up if you fully understand, a thumbs down if you need things explained a different way, and a thumb in the middle if you are somewhere in between. Keep your hand on your chest while you do this."* By keeping their hands on their chests and not raising them in the air in view for everyone, student responses will not be influenced by each other. As students are sharing their thumb check-ins, look around at their responses to gauge their self-assessed understanding.

STOP, THINK, TALK

Stop, think, talk is conducted exactly the way it sounds. During the lesson you are teaching, find a good stopping point and ask students to think about what they learned. Provide students at least 10 silent seconds to think. Giving students think or wait time can be challenging, so I recommend silently and slowly counting to 10 to allow them the time they need. Then, invite students to turn and talk with a partner in class. As students are talking, listen to their responses. As you are listening in, you will gauge their understanding to see if you need to stay the planned course or make adjustments.

STOP, THINK, JOT

"Stop, think, jot" follows the same process as "stop, think, talk." The difference is that instead of talking with a partner after thinking, students jot (write or sketch) their thinking on paper or a small whiteboard. Rather than listening in to student thinking to gauge their understanding, you will see their thinking in their jots.

NOW YOU TRY

After modeling or explaining a concept to students, using the phrase "Now you try" to invite them to give it a try is a powerful tool for formative assessment while you are teaching. As students are trying out what you just taught in the lesson, you will walk around to monitor their understanding. During the *Now You Try* period of the lesson, you might want to lean in and ask a few students about their thinking to gauge their understanding.

I ASSESSED UNDERSTANDING. NOW WHAT?

After assessing student understanding while you are teaching, it's time to make a decision. If most students are understanding your lesson or are on the path to understanding, proceed as planned. Small-group instruction or teaching the concept in a different way right after the whole-group lesson for some students might be necessary. Individual conferences or coaching might also be helpful after the lesson.

If many students are not understanding or are having a difficult time following along, it is time for you to make adjustments during the lesson. Perhaps you will choose to explain in a different way or even stop the lesson altogether to give yourself time to reflect and adjust the lesson to teach later.

Remember Ms. Vasquez from earlier? Once she realized she needed to assess for understanding during the lesson, she invited students to share their comfort level about main idea using their thumbs. As students started to adjust their thumbs, most shared a thumbs-up, four shared a thumb in the middle, and two shared a thumbs down. Ms. Vasquez took note of who needed more support and decided to gather those students in a small group to adjust her teaching for them after the lesson.

Notes

How Can I Assess if Students Are Understanding While I'm Teaching?

123

What Do I Do if I Feel a Student May Need Extra Support Outside of Classroom Time?

Since the start of the school year, Mr. Jordan noticed Dan needed extra support during reading time. He made it a point to ensure Dan always had a seat at the front of the room for lessons, conferred with Dan each day to provide individualized instruction, included him in supportive small groups and stations with encouraging peers, and provided extra guidance when Dan selected books. Despite all of his efforts, Mr. Jordan realized that Dan was still not getting what he needed as a reader. After trying a few more instructional strategies in class, Mr. Jordan reached out to Dan's parents to learn more history about him as a reader. Dan's parents and Mr. Jordan agreed that consulting the school reading specialist was the logical next step to provide Dan the support he needed.

The best advice on teaching that I've received in all my years is to first *look in the mirror, not the microscope* when teaching plans do not unfold as expected. This is exactly what Mr. Jordan did when trying to provide Dan with the support he needed. He first did everything within his control in the classroom, using Tier 1 instruction (see p. 64), before seeking potential outside support for Dan. He tried multiple instructional strategies and made changes as needed when working with Dan. Mr. Jordan realized he needed to include Dan's parents in the process of supporting him as a reader. Mr. Jordan and Dan's parents then decided to bring in another team member to figure out next steps.

After trying everything you know as a teacher, like Mr. Jordan, sometimes you'll need to bring in other team members to support you in providing the instruction your students need to grow as readers. Oftentimes, other team members, such as the school reading specialist, will provide advice on Tier 1 instructional strategies and will even come into your classroom to observe and offer feedback. Listening to feedback from other professionals helps all teachers grow and refine their practice. Sometimes, all you will need is an adjustment in your instructional practice to help a child progress. Other times, consultation with team members will lead to a more formal process if it is determined your student will benefit from further support outside of your classroom.

STEPS TO SEEKING EXTRA SUPPORT FOR STUDENTS

1   *Look in the mirror, not the microscope.* Ask yourself what you can do in the classroom before assuming that a student might need more support outside of the classroom. Try different strategies and instructional methods within the classroom first. If one doesn't work, try another, and then another.

2   *Include parents and caregivers.* The parents and caregivers of your students know them better than anyone else. They must be actively consulted and included as partners in your work, especially when their children need extra support. They will be able to offer insights and information that will be invaluable throughout the entire process.

3   *Seek out advice and support from other team members.* Your grade-level partners, reading specialist, learning specialist, instructional coach, principal, and other team members at your school can support you in providing valuable next steps. It is the responsibility of every team member at school to support all the children in the school. Seeking out support from others is not a sign of weakness; rather, it is sometimes the best route to take to provide students with the reading support they need.

4   *Continue to implement Tier 1 instruction to support your students.* If your school team ultimately determines that one of your students will receive Tier 2 or Tier 3 instruction, it is crucial that you still provide the Tier 1 classroom instruction that your student needs. Tier 2 and Tier 3 instruction are additional support, but they are not replacements for good Tier 1 instruction inside the classroom.

5   *Throughout the process, always follow the lead of your students.* Throughout the entire process of figuring out the best way to support your students, always keep their identity, strengths, and needs at the front of your decision-making. When in doubt, always look to your students as guides.

Notes

What Do I Do if I Feel a Student May Need Extra Support Outside of Classroom Time?

ASSESSMENT

125

HOW DO I SHIFT AGENCY TO STUDENTS, ENGAGING AND EMPOWERING THEM AS READERS?

During a visit to Mr. Chin's classroom in my days as a literacy coach, I watched as he ended a lesson by setting his students up for independence during work time. Right before he dismissed his students from the meeting area after the lesson, he reminded them, "Remember, right before you stand up and move to your reading area for independent reading time, make a mental list using your fingers as your checklist for how you will start your reading time." He then held up his hand, lifted his index finger, and said, "First, I will. . . ." Then, he held up his second finger and said, "Next, I will . . ."—and so on. Mr. Chin continued, "If you need my support, please wait until I am done working with my current group, but remember, you can always turn to a friend or find a way to help yourself." I then watched all of his students go through the mental process of creating their lists. One by one, they used their fingers to make their lists, stood up with their books and notebooks in hand, and walked off to start reading.

Mr. Chin had been working from the start of the school year to set his students up for independence. These small reminders given at the end of lessons were just one way he did so. The more Mr. Chin did this, in addition to implementing a few other methods, the more agency his students displayed throughout the school year.

This chapter focuses on ways you can shift agency in reading to your students, much like Mr. Chin did. You will learn about the role that engagement plays in student independence, along with how to encourage more student decision-making, and about some high-impact classroom conditions and activities that promote independence in reading.

Seven of Your Biggest Questions About How to Shift Agency to Students, Engaging and Empowering Them as Readers

1. What is student agency in reading?

2. What role does engagement play in agency?

3. What are different ways I can provide choice to students?

4. What are some ways I can encourage student feedback and decision-making?

5. What are some high-impact conditions and activities that promote student agency?

6. How can I support students in reflecting on their strengths and next steps as readers?

7. What are some ways I can support students' authentic responses to reading?

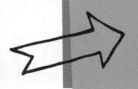

What Is Student Agency in Reading?

Agency refers to people making their own independent choices and acting of their own free will to complete tasks and solve problems. In the reading classroom, agency is something we can support students in building over time.

The first step to becoming truly agentive readers is for students to feel an authentic purpose for reading. Sometimes, that purpose is to be entertained. Other times, it is to learn something. In the classroom, another big purpose for reading is to continue to grow and develop as a reader. Agentive readers do not read because their teacher is requiring it; this is what compliant readers do. Agentive readers read because it is something they truly want to do and know that it will help them grow as people both inside and outside of school. One of your major, constant goals as a reading teacher will be to support your students in becoming truly agentive readers.

Compliant Readers . . .	Agentive Readers . . .
Typically only read when told to by a teacher	Read without being directed
Read books based on their teacher's requirements	Intentionally choose their own reading material, based on their interests and needs
Read outside of school to fulfill a requirement	Read outside of school because they want to
Depend on their teacher to tell them what to think about their reading	Value their own ideas about reading

Notes

_____

_____

_____

_____

_____

_____

_____

_____

_____

_____

What Role Does Engagement Play in Agency?

For classroom PE time, Ms. Reyes had traditionally required students to run laps around the playground because that fulfilled the state PE minutes requirement, even though it caused groaning, annoyance, and dread for some students. During one of these running sessions, one of her students stopped running and asked why she couldn't play games during PE like the other classes. Ms. Reyes thought for a moment and replied, "Well, I don't know of many PE games. Do you think you could teach the class a game?" Her student became so excited at this request that Ms. Reyes called to her class to stop running. She stepped back and allowed the student to teach a game to the class. Over the next 15 minutes, Ms. Reyes watched a class transformed. Her students who'd been grimacing just 20 minutes ago were now running around with smiles, laughing and shouting words of strategy and affirmation to each other, playing the game they just learned. In that moment, Ms. Reyes decided it was time to make a change and allow students more choice and decision-making in her class in order to increase their engagement.

In that one 15-minute PE game, Ms. Reyes's students made decisions, collaborated, grappled intellectually with different strategies, and found success with some of those strategies. They did not look to Ms. Reyes to make their decisions or for help. They did all of these things independently and also with each other.

Much like Ms. Reyes's students during PE, when students are engaged in what they are doing, they are more likely to want to repeat it. When students want to do something, they will voluntarily do it more often and seek out more time to do it— which leads to agency. The way Ms. Reyes's students smiled, laughed, and shared strategies with each other is something that can be replicated in any subject area in school, especially in reading. We know that reading volume and time spent reading independently lead to higher reading achievement. In order to meet those volume and time milestones, children need to be engaged with reading. Good news! There are specific things you can do to increase reading engagement.

What Fosters Engagement?

- Create an environment that promotes student choice and decision-making.

- Establish classroom procedures that will set up students for success.

- Model what productive struggle looks, sounds, and feels like—then, encourage it.

- Encourage curiosity and questions rather than answers and absolutes.

- Offer opportunities for collaboration, but don't force it.

AGENCY

WAYS TO INCREASE ENGAGEMENT IN READING

CREATE AN ENVIRONMENT THAT PROMOTES STUDENT CHOICE AND DECISION-MAKING

When students feel comfortable and safe in a classroom, they are more likely to freely engage in decision-making and the intellectual grapple that leads to deep learning. A comfortable and safe environment does not necessarily need to include cute decorations or fancy, expensive seating. Rather, it refers to a space where students feel welcome physically, emotionally, and intellectually. To better understand how to create a safe and welcome space, consider these questions:

- Is my classroom furniture comfortably spaced for students' physical needs?
- Are there spaces for both collaborative and independent reading?
- How am I letting students know that their thoughts and feelings about reading are valid and matter?
- Do my teaching and classroom book selection meet the intellectual needs of all my students?

ESTABLISH CLASSROOM PROCEDURES THAT WILL SET UP STUDENTS FOR SUCCESS

Setting up consistent classroom routines and procedures with students will help them free up their energy *and* your energy to focus on reading. After you set up procedures with students, they will know what to do on their own in different situations and scenarios. Successful reading classrooms with engaged readers typically have these consistent and predictable procedures and routines:

- When and how to choose books
- Where to store books and other reading materials
- Where to read
- What to do when stuck

MODEL WHAT PRODUCTIVE STRUGGLE LOOKS, SOUNDS, AND FEELS LIKE—THEN, ENCOURAGE IT

Engaged readers productively struggle with strategies and ideas when they are reading (Hammond, 2015). Productive struggle refers to students working and growing within their zone of proximal development (Vygotsky, 1978). If students find no intellectual struggle in their reading, they may become bored and disinterested. If their struggle is not productive—that is, if it is just hard and frustrating—they are likely to give up.

One way you can model productive struggle for students is to verbally share your thinking with them while reading aloud. Share how you undertake and grapple with a new strategy. Point out that trying a new strategy is not always easy. When you model productive struggle for students, they are more likely to willingly engage in it and make it a part of their everyday learning.

ENCOURAGE CURIOSITY AND QUESTIONS RATHER THAN ANSWERS AND ABSOLUTES

Students become more engaged when they are invited to inquire rather than when they are expected to know all the answers. One way to start to do this is to connect learning inside the classroom to the world outside the classroom. Students also become more engaged in reading when what they are offered to read is relevant to their own lives and taps into their curiosity about what is going on in the world outside of the classroom.

OFFER OPPORTUNITIES FOR COLLABORATION, BUT DON'T FORCE IT

Productive and effective collaboration with others is highly engaging for children. However, ineffective and forced collaboration can have the opposite effect. An example of ineffective collaboration is that group project we all remember from our own schooling—you know . . . the one where one or two students did all the work for the group of five. Or, conversely, where three students in the group of five felt unsafe because two students were taking over the project without considering everyone's input. Collaboration is only effective if all students feel safe and welcome when taking part in the group learning. Strategically creating student partnerships and triads is a key to building engagement in the reading classroom.

Great Resource

Engaging Children by Elin Keene [Heinemann, 2018]

Notes

AGENCY

What Are Different Ways I Can Provide Choice to Students?

Providing students with opportunities to make their own choices throughout the school day enables them to continually tap into their own power as independent decision-makers. Just like with book choice (see p. 49–53), how to make sound choices is a skill that needs to be directly taught in the classroom. In addition to teaching and offering book choice to students, you can also offer students choices during reading that concern where to sit, partnerships and groups, and book clubs. Here's how.

CHOICE OF WHERE TO SIT

The physical classroom environment should provide many seating options for young readers. Some prefer to sit in a traditional chair, while others may be more comfortable on the floor, leaning against a wall, or in a beanbag chair. Others may choose to stand or might need more flexibility to move a bit. The key to supporting students in choosing where to sit is to invite them to try different seating choices and determine which one feels the most successful for them. Different students will feel more comfortable and more successful in different spots.

These are just a few of many possible seating options during reading. When settling in to read a good book, fifth-grader Dash prefers to sprawl on the floor, first-grader Mateo likes to crouch on the floor with his book box, second-grader Alexander is most comfortable reading at his desk, and fourth-grader Amelia likes to sit cross-legged on the floor.

CHOICE OF PARTNERSHIPS AND GROUPS

Working with others offers many decision-making opportunities for young readers. Partnerships and groups provide students with the opportunity not only to make decisions but also to discuss and problem-solve the decision-making process together. Some of the decisions and choices for students to discuss and negotiate include these:

- What will we talk about?
- Who will talk first?
- Who will talk next?
- Will we need a note-taker?
- How can we respectfully disagree with each other?

The more students make decisions together as a group or partnership, the more comfortable they will become with making their own choices when faced with different options.

Alexander and Sam are in a reading partnership. They read together and chat about their books during supported independent reading time.

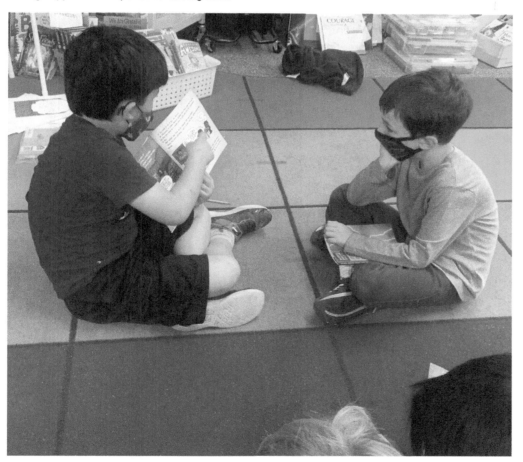

CHOICE OF BOOK CLUBS

Much like partnerships and groups, book clubs provide students ample opportunity for discussion and decision-making with others. In addition to the decision-making opportunities mentioned with groups and partnerships, students have the opportunity to share their thinking and ideas with others around a common text (for more on book clubs, see Book Clubs, p. 89).

MAKING CHOICE A SUCCESSFUL ENDEAVOR

- **What works best for me?** Invite students to think about this question as they make choices in the classroom. What works best for one student may not work well for another, so supporting students in discovering what works best for each of them will be a big help. Students might need to try a few options before they figure out the best option. This will likely take time and a bit of ongoing practice and prompting.

- **Start with limited choice at first.** Offering choice without restrictions can be overwhelming, especially if students are not yet accustomed to making choices for themselves. Rather than offering absolute free choice, offer two to three specific choices at first. For example, instead of inviting students to sit wherever they want, invite them to sit at their desk, in the library, or on a beanbag chair. Sometimes, limited choice is a good starting point to build comfort and experience with decision-making.

Notes

What Are Some Ways I Can Encourage Student Feedback and Decision-Making?

Years ago, during an independent reading time in class, a student named Annie told me that she created a book waiting list on the whiteboard at the front of the classroom. She explained that she was tired of watching Lin read the book she was waiting for. So she just decided to write the book's title on the board and wrote her name under it. Annie asked if she could invite the rest of the class to do the same for the books they were waiting for. After Annie made the announcement to the class, two other students wrote book titles and their names on the section of the whiteboard Annie labeled *Book Waiting Lists*. A couple of days later, Lin finished the book and walked it over to Annie at the beginning of the school day.

Annie felt safe writing on the classroom whiteboard without asking for my permission first. She felt safe because that was the tone established in the classroom. Students knew that the classroom was not mine, but ours. They knew because I directly told them. Is it that simple to just tell students that the classroom is ours rather than mine? Yes and no. Telling students "this is your classroom" is simple. Acting on those words takes a bit more effort. In my experience, the biggest effort requires taking a step back and allowing students to lead and make decisions for their own learning.

When stepping back and inviting students to take the lead by making their own decisions, mistakes and blunders will be made. Student-initiated decision-making is messy—just as messy as adult decision-making! I let my students in on this secret: Not only do I tell them that the classroom is ours rather than mine, but I also tell them that the practice of making the classroom ours will be messy and to expect imperfection.

Keep in Mind

Choice and decision-making are messy endeavors. Both you and your students will make mistakes. Mistakes are an opportunity to make a needed change!

Making It Yours *and* Theirs

Once the tone in the classroom is established, a few simple adjustments can help you to continue to encourage student feedback and decision-making with the goal of making the classroom collectively belong to you *and* your students.

AGENCY

What Are Some Ways I Can Encourage Student Feedback and Decision-Making?

135

In the Classroom Library

- Ask students for suggestions to make book browsing more accessible.
- Ask students which books are missing from the library that they'd like included.
- Invite students to create book baskets of their own design for the classroom library.

These book baskets were created by students in a first-grade and fifth-grade classroom.

With Small-Group and Whole-Group Lessons

- Invite students to suggest a small-group topic. Ask them what they would like to learn or discuss.
- During and after whole-group lessons, check for understanding. If you need to switch gears, let students know you are doing so based on their feedback.
- Later in the school year, invite students to teach a small-group lesson on a topic they are comfortable with.

During Reading Conferences

- Start the conference by asking, "What would you like to discuss today?"
- Practice listening to students more than talking.
- Invite students to set a goal for themselves. Support them in making a plan to work toward that goal.

During independent reading time, Keona had trouble settling in to read. She switched between rustling through her desk, shifting in her seat, and then trying to focus on the books in her book bag. Ms. Rocha noticed this and decided to have a quick conference with Keona to learn more. As she sat down next to Keona, she gently said, "Hi, Keona. I noticed you're having some trouble getting into your reading today. Do you think you can try something to help yourself?" Keona explained to Ms. Rocha that she was just uncomfortable at her desk and should find a different spot for reading. Ms. Rocha responded with, "That sounds like a good plan you just made for yourself." Then, off Keona went to sit in the cozy reading corner, her focus sustained, reading the books in her book bag for the remainder of the time.

By inviting Keona to help herself rather than stepping in to help her, Ms. Rocha positioned Keona to take charge of her own situation. This also showed Keona that each time she becomes distracted or uncomfortable, she can solve the issue herself by making her own plan. Setting up the condition for student self-selected seating was a strategic choice made by Ms. Rocha. There are also a few other strategic conditions you can create to promote student agency.

PROMOTING STUDENT AGENCY

REFRAME TEACHING LANGUAGE TO BE STUDENT-FOCUSED RATHER THAN TEACHER-FOCUSED

For my first 10 years as a teacher, the language I used was well-intended but dominantly teacher-focused. When I started working as a literacy coach, I began to question the language I used. Making a few simple swaps was all that was needed to switch my own language from teacher-focused to student-focused. The trick to this is removing the word "I" when addressing students and swapping it out for the word "you." To get started thinking about the language you use, try some of the following language swaps to make your language about the reader instead of about the teacher.

Common Teacher-Focused Phrase	Student-Centered Phrase
I'm so proud of you!	You should feel proud of yourself!
I like what you just said.	You just said something so wise.
I like the way you read all the sounds in that word.	You just read all the sounds in that word.
I will help you.	What can you try to help yourself?

AGENCY

IDENTIFY DIFFERENT REASONS WHY PEOPLE INDEPENDENTLY READ

After naming different reasons why people read, invite students to think about how this looks in their own life. When students can identify an authentic purpose for themselves to read, they will be more likely to read of their own volition. Take a look at this chart from a second-grade classroom with student comments about why they read.

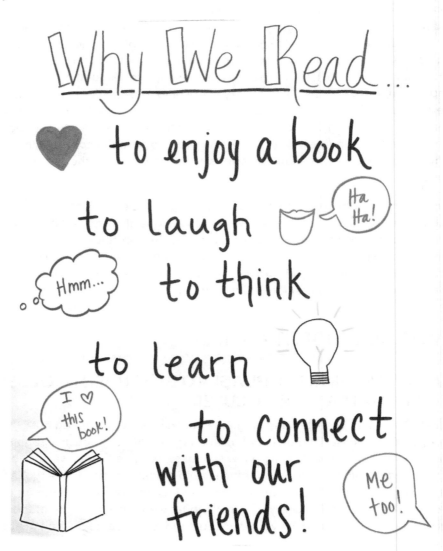

POINT OUT TO STUDENTS WHEN YOU SEE THEM BEING AGENTIVE

When a student is taking the initiative to do something new or something that will benefit them if it's repeated, let them know! When we notice and name what students are doing, they are likely to repeat it (Johnston, 2004). It can be as simple as a quick comment during a small group. "James, you just finished reading your new book again, so you decided on your own to start rereading a book from your book bag. Way to make that decision for yourself!" An additional benefit of doing this during small-group time or within earshot of other students is that they will hear and benefit from your noticing as well.

SUPPORT CONVERSATION BETWEEN STUDENTS WITH PROMPTS

A successful conversation between readers requires agency from all students involved. Some students will not need support in having reading discussions with other students. Others will need prompting to help them both engage in conversation and to keep the talking going. Teaching a lesson on how to have a reading conversation is a great starting point for all students. Creating a chart that students can refer to during these conversations will continue to support students who need extra support (see Charts for Student Talk, p. 28).

STRATEGICALLY CREATE NEW PARTNERSHIPS OR TRIADS WITH EACH NEW READING UNIT

To help students develop a meaningful and productive relationship with other readers in class, strategically place students in new partnerships or triads with each new reading unit or every few weeks. When students are comfortable with those they are working with, they are less likely to need teacher support with their reading conversations. A strong partner can also help students who might need a little extra push. I'm a firm believer that the adult is not the only teacher in the classroom. Students can learn a great deal from each other and even about themselves when they have to opportunity to build trusting relationships with each other. Reading partners and triads can sit together during read aloud, in reading-focused stations, and even during supported independent reading time to offer each other conversation and support when needed.

Tip

When creating student partnerships or triads, consider personality, work style, and reading strengths and needs.

INITIATE AND CONTINUALLY SUPPORT STUDENTS WITH SELF-ASSESSMENT AND GOAL SETTING

One of my favorite lessons to teach is to share with students how to set goals as a reader. To do this, you can use a document camera with your own reading notebook or chart paper to explicitly show your students what this looks and sounds like. By modeling how you reflect on what you need to work on as a reader and inviting students to do the same during the lesson, your student readers will see an example of how to independently set goals and then practice setting their own goals right after. This is something you can revisit with students in conferences and small groups. Primary students can refer to either teacher-written or self-written goal reminders on a sticky note they keep in their book bags or boxes, while upper-elementary students can keep a running list of their goals in their reading notebooks.

AGENCY

Second-grader Evie's current sticky-note goal

Evie's Goal: Read all the words on a page!

Fourth-grader Amelia's reading notebook goal-setting page

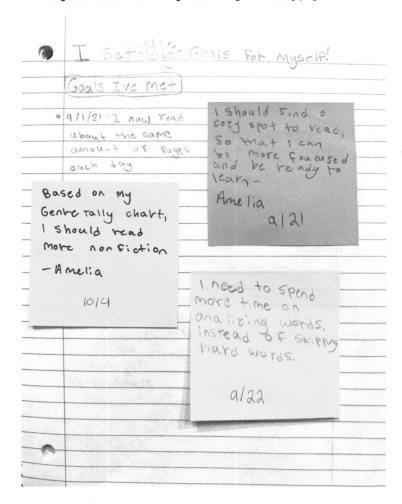

I Set Big Goals for Myself!

Goals I've Met

• 9/1/21 - I now read about the same amount of pages each day

Based on my Genre Tally chart, I should read More nonfiction
- Amelia
10/4

I should find a cozy spot to read, so that I can be more focused and be ready to learn.
- Amelia
9/21

I need to spend more time on analizing words, instead of skipping hard words.
9/22

How Can I Support Students in Reflecting on Their Strengths and Next Steps as Readers?

During a reading conference with Gino, Ms. Hill noticed that he excitedly talked about his book, but when asked about what he was working on as a reader, Gino didn't know what to say. Ms. Hill realized that most of her students didn't know what to say when she asked this question, even though they were all using reading strategies and applying skills she taught in lessons. She wanted to support her students with self-reflection, but she wasn't sure where to start.

Supporting students in naming and reflecting on their strengths and next steps as readers can be a challenge at first. There are a few methods that can be implemented to encourage self-reflection.

SUPPORTING STUDENTS AND ENCOURAGING SELF-REFLECTION

SPY ON YOURSELF AS A READER

When you spy on yourself as a reader, you are acting as a detective, seeking out the reading skills and strategies you use when you realize you are finding trouble in your reading. For example, when I was reading a new-to-me novel recently, I completely zoned out. My mind started thinking about all that I had to accomplish that day while I was still decoding the words on the page. At the end of a chapter, I had no clue about what I just read. So to help myself understand what I just read, I turned back a few pages and started skimming to find the point in the text where my mind might have started wandering outside of the book. Once I found that point, I started intently reading again, this time going slowly and stopping at the end of every few paragraphs to think about what I had just read.

SHARE YOUR OWN STRENGTHS AND NEXT STEPS AS A READER

After practicing spying on yourself as a reader, share it with your students. After this episode of my mind wandering outside of the novel I was reading, I shared it with my students. I told them that noticing what I need to work on is still part of being a reader, even at my age. "Even though I've been a skilled reader for many years, I still need to work on noticing when my thinking wanders outside of a book. What are some things you might need to work on?" When I model noticing and sharing my own struggles and successes as a reader, my students are more likely to notice and share their own as well.

How Can I Support Students in Reflecting on Their Strengths and Next Steps as Readers?

141

Display a chart like this one from a third-grade classroom of learning targets already taught. This will support students in using language to identify what they are working on as readers.

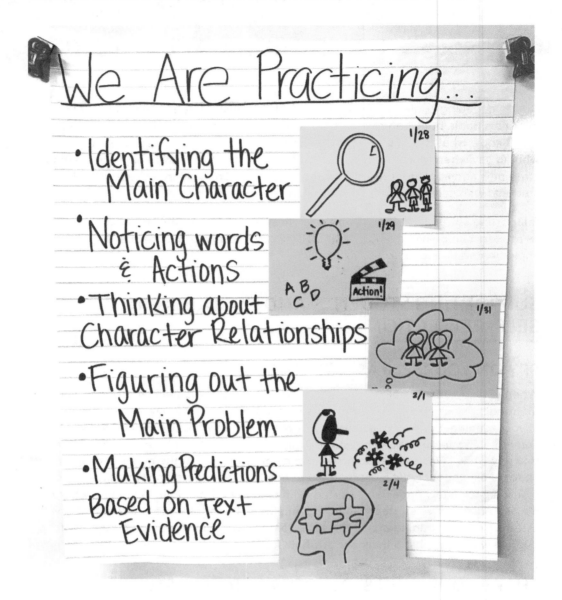

TEACH AND DISPLAY REFLECTIVE LANGUAGE PROMPTS

Beginning to use the language of reflection can be tricky, especially for our youngest readers. Using and displaying common reflective sentence starters can support your readers in their reflection work:

- A strength I have as a reader is . . .
- One thing I'm proud of is . . .
- As a reader, I am working on . . .
- As a reader, I am practicing . . .

What Are Some Ways I Can Support Students' Authentic Response to Reading?

Authentic response is how readers react to their reading, unprompted and independent of others. It is what we do as adult readers. Here are a few examples of authentic response from my own reading at the time of this writing:

- Due to reading more about the Delta variant of Covid-19, I started wearing a mask indoors again, despite being vaccinated. This is an example of taking action based on learning more information in my reading.
- I enjoyed reading *Such a Fun Age* by Kiley Reid (2019) so much that I decided to buy one of her other books. I also recommended the book to a friend and gave it to her when I finished.
- While reading an article by Nell Duke and Kelly Cartwright (2021), I took notes on ideas that were new to me and collected them in a journal to share with my colleagues.

These examples from my own authentic response to reading are all things that I decided to do on my own without any prompting from someone else. A reader who authentically responds to their reading is an agentive, engaged reader.

Keep in Mind

Common reading projects of days past, such as a diorama of a book's setting or a formulaic book report, are not forms of authentic response. If it is something students do not do or generate on their own terms, it is not authentic response.

TEACHING STUDENTS TO TAP INTO THEIR OWN AUTHENTIC RESPONSE

In our 2018 book, *To Know and Nurture a Reader*, Kari Yates and I identified three categories of authentic response:

- **Reflection:** Noticing one's own thinking and feeling during and after reading
  - Reacting while reading a book: laughing, smiling, feeling an emotion (happiness, relief, sadness, etc.)
  - Jotting thoughts, ideas, and wonderings
  - Realizing something about oneself due to reading

AGENCY

- **Connection:** Making connections with other readers and people
  - Talking with friends in the moment
  - Recommending a book to a friend after reading
  - Learning about different people in the community and world

- **Action:** Deciding to do something as a result of what was read
  - Choosing whether to continue or abandon the book
  - Deciding to use a text as a mentor for writing
  - Changing behavior or taking a specific action

Some students might not automatically authentically respond to reading on their own. Or they might not know that their authentic responses are valued in the classroom. Consider teaching a lesson or two about ways readers authentically respond to texts. The chart seen here is from a third-grade discussion with students about authentic response to reading.

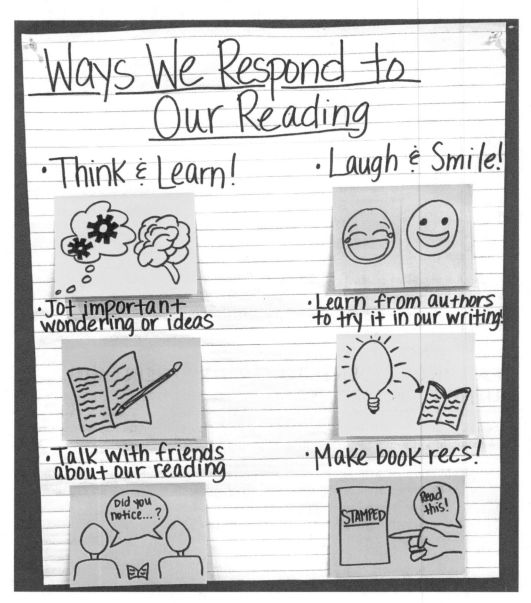

chapter SIX

WHERE DO I GO FROM HERE?

As I finish writing this book, I am well into my 20th year as a teacher. It has been two decades since my dear mentor Midge took me under her wing and introduced me to professional reading and the many literacy leaders I still follow to this day. Across these past 20 years, many new leaders and pieces of research in the teaching of reading have emerged. One thing I know for certain is that change is inevitable. It is something all teachers need to expect and accept. However, two things that haven't changed in those 20 years are my values for teaching reading and my drive to learn and grow. While you will always hold tight to your values, embrace the ever-changing landscape that is literacy education, especially in the teaching of reading.

START SMALL FOR BIG GAINS

To continue your learning journey, consider your next logical step. Perhaps you are ready to commit to a daily conferring practice. Maybe you'd like to focus on incorporating more intentional phonemic awareness into your daily routine. Or you might want to spend some time working on getting to know your students and building a community of supportive readers. Whatever your area of focus, start small to achieve big gains. Pick one thing to start with and commit to it.

You might also consider starting your next professional read to help you out in the process. Flip back to the question that will support you with getting started in your focus area. If there are *Great Resources* listed there, pick one to read to start learning more.

Each of the authors in the listed *Great Resources* has also written other books—plus, there are many more whom I haven't listed. When you're ready for more in-depth learning, seek out these educator–authors and others to grow your reading practice in your classroom.

CONNECT WITH OTHERS

Connecting with other educators committed to continually growing is a way to remain motivated and enhance your professional learning. If your school has a literacy coach, that's a great place to start. You can also turn to like-minded colleagues at your school site. Ask other teachers if they'd like to join you on your journey to grow as a reading teacher. You'll never know if someone wants to join you until you ask! Additionally, try to watch others teach reading. I always learn so much more about the teaching of reading when I have the opportunity to observe in another teacher's classroom.

Believe it or not, Twitter is also a great place to seek out support. There is a very active literacy education community on Twitter. If Twitter is new to you, a good starting place on Twitter is the #G2Great chat every Thursday evening to start to learn from and connect with other teachers and literacy education leaders.

Joining a professional organization is another fantastic way to keep growing. There are a plethora of local, state, and national professional organizations devoted to literacy education. The National Council of Teachers of English (NCTE) has become my professional home over the past decade. They offer countless opportunities to connect both virtually and in-person with other like-minded educators.

Ask colleagues, as well, about local and regional professional organizations they enjoy, such as those affiliated with the International Literacy Association (ILA), and find out more about reading-focused conferences such as Literacy for All and LitCon.

Colleagues, literacy coaches, and teachers you meet in online spaces can tell you, too, about journals, blogs, and podcasts they find valuable. Opportunities for professional connection abound! The best way to continue to grow is to keep connecting with educators who share your values and are committed to this journey as well.

THE NEXT STEPS

You've now taken the step to commit to learning more about the teaching of reading. You've got this! You will make mistakes along the way—I still make them as a veteran teacher. Don't be afraid to mess up. Learning and growing are supposed to be messy! The key is recognizing when it happens and taking the steps to do better next time.

As Midge instilled in me so many years ago, learning is a careerlong endeavor, and it's a magical one! I'm so glad you're joining me and the many other dedicated literacy educators across the world for the ride. By committing to continually learning and growing as a teacher of reading, you are truly committing to your students. There is nothing more important than that.

Notes

Appendix Contents

A. Interest Survey K–1 (Ch. 1, Q2: p. 14)

B. Interest Survey 2–3 (Ch. 1, Q2: p. 14)

C. Interest Survey 4–5 (Ch. 1, Q2: p. 14)

D. Teacher Observation Survey (Ch. 1, Q2: p. 14)

E. Online Sources for Children's Literature (Ch. 1, Q4: p. 18; Ch. 2, Q5: p. 47, Q9: p. 60)

F. Common Questions and Concerns From Parents and Caregivers (Ch. 1, Q7: p. 29)

G. Weekly Reading Instructional Plan (Ch. 2, Q9: p. 60)

H. Class List With Checkboxes (Ch. 4, Q4: p. 111)

I. Reading Three Goals Formative Assessment Form (Ch. 4, Q4: p. 111)

J. Individual Assessment Form (Ch. 4, Q4: p. 111)

All of these items are available for download from the book's companion website, **resources.corwin.com/answerselementaryreading**

Appendix A. Grades K–1 Reading Interest Survey and Teacher Directions

As a kindergarten or first-grade teacher, the best way to get to know your students as readers is to read with them and watch them interact with books over time.

Strategically using this survey will also help you learn a little bit more about each of your readers. Depending on the strengths and needs of each of your students, you might decide to use this survey as either an individual, small-group, or whole-group activity.

- *Individual*: You will likely write each of your students' verbal responses on the Student Page. Use one copy per student.
- *Small Group*: You will pass out the Student Page to each student in the group, give the following prompts, and offer support as needed.
- *Whole Group*: You will pass out the Student Page to each student in class, give the following prompts, and offer support as needed.

To administer the Interest Survey, you can use these prompts as a guide. Adjust as needed, based on your students.

1. *Right now, I want to learn more about you as a reader.*
2. *I'm going to ask you to draw or write in the two boxes on this paper.* (If recording student responses, instead say, *I'm going to ask you three questions.*) Then, be ready to jot down student answers in each box.
3. *In the box on the top, draw or write a picture of yourself reading.* Give students ample time to show their thinking through pictures and/or words. (If recording student responses, you might ask, *Do you like to read? Tell me all about it.*)
4. *In the box on the bottom, draw or write a few of your favorite things.* Give students ample time to show their thinking through pictures and/or words. (If recording student responses, you might ask, *What are some of your favorite things and things you like to do?*)
5. Once students are finished, collect their surveys. If needed, ask students to tell you a little bit about what they wrote or drew. Use the information to inform your reading instructional planning and decisions.

Name _____

This Is Me Reading

Some of My Favorite Things

Appendix B. Grades 2–3 Reading Interest Survey

Name _____ Date _____

Circle a Thumb for Each One

| I like to read at school. | 👍 | ✋ | 👎 |
| I like to read when I'm not at school. | 👍 | ✋ | 👎 |

Write or Draw

My Favorite Things . . .	My Favorite Books . . .

Appendix C. Grades 4–5 Reading Interest Survey

Name _____ Date _____

Check the box that matches most with your thinking about your reading life.

Reading Life Statement	Agree	Not Sure	Disagree
I enjoy reading.			
I'm currently reading a book I'm enjoying.			
I know how to find books that interest me.			
I look forward to reading when I'm not reading.			
I already know a book I want to read next.			

Complete each statement.

A few books I've enjoyed are . . .
I would like to read books about . . .
Reading works best for me when . . .

Appendix D. Teacher Observation Survey

Student Name _____ **Dates** _____

Book Choice Observations

Date	Date	Date

Date	Date	Date

Reading Engagement and Stamina Observations

Date	Date	Date

Date	Date	Date

Answers to Your Biggest Questions About Teaching Elementary Reading

Small-Group and Whole-Group Observations

Date	Date	Date

Date	Date	Date

Conferring (1:1) Observations

Date	Date	Date

Date	Date	Date

Appendix E. Online Sources for Learning About and Staying Informed on Children's Literature

Awards to Follow

Asian/Pacific American Award for Literature: http://www.apalaweb.org/awards/literature-awards/

Charlotte Huck Award: https://ncte.org/awards/ncte-childrens-book-awards/charlotte-huck-award/

Coretta Scott King Book Awards: https://www.ala.org/rt/emiert/cskbookawards

John Newbery Medal: https://www.ala.org/alsc/awardsgrants/bookmedia/newbery

NCTE Award for Excellence in Children's Poetry: https://ncte.org/awards/excellence-in-poetry-for-children-living-american-poet/

Orbis Pictus Award: https://ncte.org/awards/orbis-pictus-award-nonfiction-for-children/

Pura Belpré Award: https://www.ala.org/alsc/awardsgrants/bookmedia/belpre

Randolph Caldecott Medal: https://www.ala.org/alsc/awardsgrants/bookmedia/caldecott

Stonewall Book Awards: https://www.ala.org/rt/rrt/award/stonewall

Blogs and Websites

Brown Bookshelf: https://thebrownbookshelf.com/

Clare Landrigan's Virtual Bookroom: https://www.clarelandrigan.com/

The Horn Book Inc: https://www.hbook.com/

Nerdy Book Club: https://nerdybookclub.wordpress.com/

We Need Diverse Books: https://diversebooks.org/

Instagram

@heisereads, Jillian Heise

@textsets, Franki Sibberson

@thetututeacher, Vera Ahiyya

Appendix F. Common Questions and Concerns From Parents and Caregivers About Reading

Is it OK that my child reads the same books over and over?

Re-reading the same book over and over provides comfort and familiarity for children. It has the potential to help children build fluency and become familiar with story structure. Children get plenty of opportunity to read a variety of material at school. It's OK if they choose to read the same books over and over again at home. They will eventually find interest in new books and reading material as they grow and learn more.

How can I challenge my child in reading?

Rather than looking to challenge your child in reading, consider looking to foster their love of reading. Frequent trips to the local library and reading books together are great starts!

My child only reads graphic novels and comics.

Graphic novels and comics are excellent forms of reading material! If your child enjoys them, encourage it! Perhaps try reading a graphic novel or comic with your child. Highly visual texts like these offer the opportunity for children to read and understand both images and words. Our world and the reading material in it are only becoming more and more visual with time. We need to support kids in navigating it, and graphic novels and comics are a great start. Plus, these texts are also an entry point for growing a love of reading for many children.

My child doesn't like to read.

This is always challenging. When a child does not enjoy reading, reading material is often the culprit. Allowing children to choose their own reading material and supporting them in doing so will likely make a big difference. Spending time once a week at the local library and working with your child to find books they *can* read and *want* to read might help. Also, if you're not already in the habit, make a little time each day to read with your child; choose a book together and then carve out 15 to 20 minutes to enjoy the story together. Many families do this right before bedtime as part of a routine.

Dates _____ **Current Reading Unit** _____

Whole-Group Lessons	
Monday	
Tuesday	
Wednesday	
Thursday	
Friday	

Read Alouds	Interactive	For Enjoyment or Other Reason
Monday		
Tuesday		
Wednesday		
Thursday		
Friday		

Stations This Week			

Small Groups	Students	Instructional Focus
Monday		
Tuesday		
Wednesday		
Thursday		
Friday		

Reading Conferences	
Monday	
Tuesday	
Wednesday	
Thursday	
Friday	

1.									
2.									
3.									
4.									
5.									
6.									
7.									
8.									
9.									
10.									
11.									
12.									
13.									
14.									
15.									
16.									
17.									
18.									
19.									
20.									
21.									
22.									
23.									
24.									
25.									
26.									
27.									
28.									
29.									
30.									

Notes:

Appendix I: Reading Three Goals Formative Assessment Form

Reading Unit _____ **Date(s)** _____

Pencil in student names in the appropriate column, based on formative assessment from observations, conferences, and small groups. As students show growth, move their names to the next column.

	Habit/Strategy/Skill	Habit/Strategy/Skill	Habit/Strategy/Skill
Student consistently demonstrates this habit, strategy, or skill.			
Almost there. Evidence is present, but use is not consistent yet.			
Evidence is not present yet.			
Need more information. The evidence is unclear.			

Appendix J: Individual Student Assessment Form

Student Name _____ Dates _____

Area of Focus:	Area of Focus:
Area of Focus:	**Area of Focus:**

REFERENCES

Ahmed, S. (2018). *Being the change: Lessons and strategies to teach social comprehension.* Heinemann.

Ahmed, S., & Daniels, H. (2014). *Upstanders: How to engage middle school hearts and minds with inquiry.* Heinemann.

Allen, L., Snow, E., & McNamara, D. (2015). Are you reading my mind? Modeling students' reading comprehension skills with natural language processing techniques. *LAK '15: Proceedings of the Fifth International Conference on Learning Analytics and Knowledge,* 246–254. https://doi.org/10.1145/2723576.2723617

Allington, D. (2012). *What really matters for struggling readers: Designing research-based programs.* Pearson.

Anderson, R. C., Wilson, P. T., & Fielding, L. G. (1988). How children spend their time outside of school. *Reading Research Quarterly, 23*(3), 285–303.

Beers, K., & Probst, R. (2017). *Disrupting thinking: Why how we read matters.* Scholastic.

Bialystok, E. (2006). The impact of bilingualism on language and literacy development. In T. K. Bhatia & W. E. Ritchie (Eds.), *The handbook of bilingualism* (pp. 577–601). Blackwell.

Brady, S. (2020). A 2020 perspective on research findings on alphabetics (phoneme awareness and phonics): Implications for instruction. *The Reading League Journal, 1*(3), 20–28.

Burkins, J., & Yaris, K. (2016). *Who's doing the work: How to say less so readers can do more.* Stenhouse.

Calkins, L. (2015). *A guide to the reading workshop: Primary grades.* Heinemann.

Calkins, L. (2017). *A guide to the reading workshop: Intermediate grades.* Heinemann.

Cherry-Paul, S., & Johansen, D. (2019). *Breathing new life into book clubs: A practical guide for teachers.* Heinemann.

Chin, N. B., & Wigglesworth, G. (2007). *Bilingualism: An advanced resource book.* Routledge.

Clay, M. (2000). *Concepts about print: What have children learned about the way we print language?* Heinemann.

Clay, M. (2017). *Running records for classroom teachers* (2nd ed.). Heinemann.

Collins, K., & Glover, M. (2015). *I am reading: Nurturing young children's meaning making and joyful engagement with any book.* Heinemann.

Cruz, M. C. (2018). *Writers read better: Nonfiction, 50+ paired lessons that turn writing craft work into powerful genre reading.* Corwin.

Cruz, M. C. (2019). *Writers read better: Narrative, 50+ paired lessons that turn writing craft work into powerful genre reading.* Corwin.

Darling-Hammond, L. (2001). *The right to learn: A blueprint for creating schools that work.* Jossey-Bass.

Diller, D. (2020). *Simply stations: Independent reading.* Corwin.

Diller, D. (2021). *Simply small groups: Differentiating literacy learning in any setting.* Corwin.

Draper, S. (2018). *Blended.* Atheneum Books for Young Readers.

Duke, N., & Cartwright, K. (2021). Science of reading progresses again. *Reading Research Quarterly, 56*(S1), S25–S44.

Dweck, C. (2014, November). *The power of believing that you can improve* [Video]. TED Conferences. https://www.ted.com/talks/carol_dweck_the_power_of_believing_that_you_can_improve

España, C., & Herrera, L. (2020). *En comunidad: Lessons for centering the voices and experiences of bilingual Latinx students.* Heinemann.

Fisher, D., Frey, N., & Akhavan, N. (2019). *This is balanced literacy, grades K–6.* Corwin.

Fountas, I., & Pinnell, G. S. (2016). *Guided reading* (2nd ed.). Heinemann.

Gardiner, J. R., & Sewall, M. (1980). *Stone fox.* Scholastic.

Goodman, Y., & Owacki, G. (2002). *Kidwatching: Documenting children's literacy development.* Heinemann.

Gough, P., & Tunmer, W. (1986). Decoding, reading, and reading disability. *Remedial and Special Education, 7*(1), 6–10.

Graves, D. H., & Murray, D. M. (1980). Revision: In the writer's workshop and in the classroom. *Journal of Education, 162*(2), 38–56.

Haberman, M. (1991). The pedagogy of poverty versus good teaching. *Phi Delta Kappan, 73*(4), 290–294.

Hammond, Z. (2015). *Culturally responsive teaching and the brain: Promoting authentic engagement and rigor among culturally and linguistically diverse students.* Corwin.

Heise, J. *Classroom book a day* website. https://www.heisereads.com/blog/

Howard, M. (2012). *Good to great teaching: Focusing on literacy work that matters.* Heinemann.

Jiménez, L. *BookToss: No easy book love* website. https://booktoss.org/

Johnston, P. (2003). *Choice words: How our language affects children's learning.* Stenhouse.

Koutrakos, P. (2018). *Word study that sticks: Best practices, K–6.* Corwin.

Krashen, S. D. (1989). We acquire vocabulary and spelling by reading: Additional evidence for the input hypothesis. *The Modern Language Journal, 73*, 440–464.

Laminack, L. (2016). *The ultimate read-aloud resource: Making every moment intentional and instructional with best friend books.* Scholastic.

Learning for Justice. (n.d.). Test yourself for hidden bias. https://www.learningforjustice.org/professional-development/test-yourself-for-hidden-bias

Lee, L. (2020). *The Mindy Kim collection, books 1–6.* Aladdin.

Loftus, M., & Sappington, L. (Hosts). (2021, July 30). Re-thinking the reading rope with Nell Duke (No. 66) [Audio podcast episode]. In *Melissa and Lori Love Literacy.* Literacy Podcast.

McVee, M. B., Dunsmore, K., & Gavelek, J. R. (2005). Schema theory revisited. *Review of Educational Research, 75*(4), 531–566.

Miller, D. (2009). *The book whisperer: Awakening the inner reader in every child.* Jossey-Bass.

Miller, D., & Moss, B. (2013). *No more independent reading without support.* Heinemann.

Mraz, K., Porcelli, A., & Tyler, C. (2016). *Purposeful play: A teacher's guide to igniting deep and joyful learning across the day.* Heinemann.

Muhammad, G. (2020). *Cultivating genius: An equity framework for culturally and historically responsive literacy.* Scholastic.

Nagy, W. E., Anderson, R. C., & Herman, P. A. (1987). Learning word meanings from context during normal reading. *American Educational Research Journal, 24*(2), 237–270.

Nation, I. S. P., & Coady, J. (1988). Vocabulary and reading. In R. Carter & M. McCarthy, (Eds.), *Vocabulary and language teaching* (pp. 97–110). Longman.

Nerdy book club website. https://nerdybookclub.wordpress.com/

Oakes, J. (2005). *Keeping track: How schools structure inequality.* Yale University Press.

Ozuru, Y., Dempsey, K., & McNamara, D. S. (2009, June). Prior knowledge, reading skill, and text cohesion in the comprehension of science texts. *Learning and Instruction, 19*(3), 228–242.

Pak, S., & Weseley, A. (2012). The effect of mandatory reading logs on children's motivation to read. *Journal of Research in Education, 22*(1), 251–265.

Pearson, P. D., & Gallagher, M. C. (1983). The instruction of reading comprehension. *Contemporary Educational Psychology, 8*(3), 317–344.

Pressley, M. (1998). *Reading instruction that works: The case for balanced teaching.* Guilford.

Ray, K. W. (1999). *Wondrous words: Writers and writing in the elementary classroom.* National Council of Teachers of English.

Reese, D., & Mendoza, J. (2021). *American Indians in children's literature* website. https://americanindiansinchildrensliterature.blogspot.com/

Roberts, K., & Beattie-Roberts, M. (2016). *DIY literacy: Teaching tools for differentiation, rigor, and independence.* Heinemann.

Ryan, P. M. (2000). *Esperanza rising.* Scholastic.

Scarborough, H. S. (2001). Connecting early language and literacy to later reading (dis)abilities: Evidence, theory, and practice. In S. B. Neuman & D. K. Dickinson (Eds.), *Handbook of early literacy research* (Vol. 1, pp. 97–110). Guilford.

Scoggin, J., & Schneewind, H. (2021). *Trusting readers: Powerful practices for independent reading.* Heinemann.

Sims Bishop, R. (1990). Mirrors, windows, and sliding glass doors. *Perspectives: Choosing and Using Books for the Classroom, 6*(3). https://files.eric.ed.gov/fulltext/ED337744.pdf#page=11

Stevens, E. A., Walker, M. A., & Vaughn, S. (2017). The effects of reading fluency interventions on the reading fluency and reading comprehension performance of elementary students with learning disabilities. *Journal of Learning Disabilities, 50*(5), 576–590.

Suggate, S. P. (2016). A meta-analysis of the long-term effects of phonemic awareness, phonics, fluency, and reading comprehension interventions. *Journal of Learning Disabilities, 49*(1), 77–96.

Sulzby, E. (1985). Children's emergent reading of favorite storybooks: A developmental study. *Reading Research Quarterly, 20*(4), 458–481.

Vygotsky, L. (1978). Interaction between learning and development. In *Mind in society: The development of higher psychological processes*. Harvard University Press.

Walther, M. (2018). *The ramped-up read aloud: What to notice as you turn the page*. Corwin.

Walther, M. (2022). *Shake up shared reading*. Corwin.

We need diverse books website. https://diversebooks.org/

Wiggins, G. (2012, January 11). Transfer as the point in education [Blog post]. *Granted, and. . . thoughts on education by Grant Wiggins*. https://grantwiggins.wordpress.com/2012/01/11/transfer-as-the-point-of-education/

Wright, J. (2021). *What's our response: Creating systems and structures to support all learners*. First Educational Resources.

Wright, J., & Hoonan, B. (2018). *What are you grouping for? Grades 3–8: How to guide small groups based on readers—not books*. Corwin.

Yates, K., & Nosek, C. (2018). *To know and nurture a reader: Conferring with confidence and joy*. Stenhouse.

INDEX

Because...
ALL TEACHERS ARE LEADERS

DOMINIQUE SMITH, DOUGLAS FISHER, NANCY FREY
Take an active approach toward disrupting the negative effects of labels and assumptions that interfere with student learning.

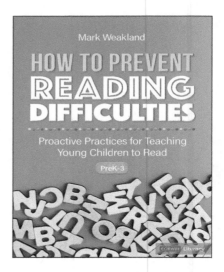

MARK WEAKLAND
Build on decades of evidence and years of experience to understand how the brain learns to read and how to apply that understanding to Tier 1 instruction.

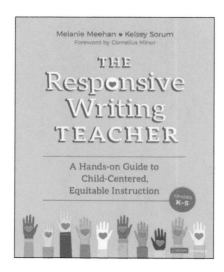

MELANIE MEEHAN, KELSEY SORUM
Learn how to adapt curriculum to meet the needs of the whole child. Each chapter offers intentional steps for responsive instruction across four domains: academic, linguistic, cultural, and social-emotional.

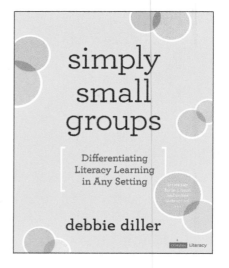

DEBBIE DILLER
Discover concrete guidance for tailoring the small-group experience to literacy instruction in order to give every reader a pathway to success.

To order your copies, visit corwin.com/literacy

At Corwin Literacy we have put together a collection of just-in-time, classroom-tested, practical resources from trusted experts that allow you to quickly find the information you need when you need it.

DOUGLAS FISHER, NANCY FREY, NICOLE LAW
Using a structured, three-pronged approach— skill, will, and thrill—students experience reading as a purposeful act with this new comprehensive model of reading instruction.

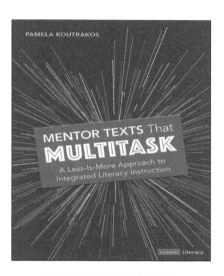

PAM KOUTRAKOS
Packed with ready-to-go lessons and tools, this user-friendly resource provides ways to weave together different aspects of literacy using one mentor text.

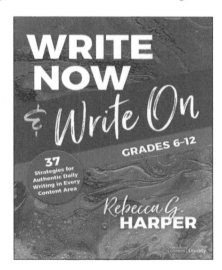

REBECCA G. HARPER
Customizable strategies turn students' informal writing into a springboard for daily writing practice in every content area—with a focus on academic vocabulary, summarizing, and using textual evidence.

MELANIE MEEHAN, CHRISTINA NOSEK, MATTHEW JOHNSON, DAVE STUART JR., MATTHEW R. KAY
This series offers actionable answers to your most pressing questions about teaching reading, writing, and ELA.

CORWIN

A SAGE Publishing Company

CORWIN HAS ONE MISSION: to enhance education through intentional professional learning.

We build long-term relationships with our authors, educators, clients, and associations who partner with us to develop and continuously improve the best evidence-based practices that establish and support lifelong learning.